Domestic Violence

A True Story of Living through
Domestic Violence

*(Powerful Story Exposes the Cruelty of Abusive
Relationships Physical)*

Charles Wheatley

Published By **Tyson Maxwell**

Charles Wheatley

Domestic Violence: A True Story of Living through Domestic Violence (Powerful Story Exposes the Cruelty of Abusive Relationships Physical)

ISBN   978-1-9992226-3-5

Legal & Disclaimer

Table Of Contents

Chapter 1: Recognizing The Signs

Understanding Abuse

Abuse can take many workplace work, together with physical, sexual, emotional, verbal, and financial mistreatment and verbal and emotional abuse. Each nation leaves an indelible mark on the sufferer's lifestyles, generating a exquisite deal ache and suffering. It is critical to maintain in mind that abuse has no limits; it can get up in non-public connections, family relationships, friendships, or perhaps expert situations. This is a few thing that everyone ought to be aware of. We lay the idea for spotting the indicators of abuse in numerous settings if we widen our know-how of what constitutes abuse.

Physical Abuse:

Physical abuse, which may be diagnosed through the scars and bruises it leaves behind, might be the maximum apparent form of maltreatment. It includes any act of violence, whether or not or now not hitting, punching, slapping, kicking, or causing bodily ache on the sufferer. It is essential to apprehend that physical pressure in competition to a few one-of-a-kind man or woman is in no way best, no matter the occasions. To find out signs and symptoms of bodily abuse, one must pay near hobby to obvious accidents, bruising that can not be rationally defined, or everyday styles of suspicious incidents. Recognizing the symptoms of physical abuse is crucial to maintaining the fitness and safety of individuals victimized through it.

Sexual Abuse:

Mistreatment that incorporates non-consensual sexual actions or exploitation can be labeled because the particularly worrying kind of abuse known as sexual abuse. It includes hundreds of behaviors, along with sexual assault, rape, coercion, unwelcome sexual advances, or any form of sexual activity imposed onto a participant who is unwilling to have interaction in it. Recognizing the signs and symptoms of sexual abuse may be especially hard due to the not unusual emotions of shame, guilt, and worry related with the victim's studies of being abused sexually. It is of the most significance to offer a setting for survivors that is unfastened from judgment and stable sufficient to percentage their studies and are looking for for assist.

Emotional Abuse:

Victims of emotional abuse go through a excellent deal of ache and struggling, and the abuse leaves at the back of unseen scars that can be simply as unstable as bodily wounds. It often lowers vanity, dignity, and everyday emotional well-being through the usage of abusive behaviors together with manipulation, intimidation, humiliation, or chronic criticism. To understand the signs of emotional abuse, one need to pay near interest to fluctuations in temper, lingering emotions of worthlessness, anxiety, disappointment, and a pervasive revel in of getting to stroll on eggshells on the equal time due to the fact the abuser is gift. Individuals get the strength to interrupt unfastened from the insidious maintain of emotional abuse once they recognize its underlying techniques.

Verbal Abuse:

The use of words in this kind of way as to disparage, belittle, humiliate, or in any other case degrade the sufferer constitutes the form of mistreatment referred to as verbal abuse. It may be insults, name-calling, shouting, continual complaint, or threatening language. Abusive language has a corrosive effect on someone's enjoy of self esteem. It can also additionally have a terrible impact on their highbrow fitness. Paying interest to conversation styles to recognize verbal abuse symptoms is important. These styles include constantly undermining the victim's self-worth, instilling fear, or manipulating words.

Financial Abuse:

Even even though it's miles a awesome device that abusers hire to exert manipulate over their patients, financial abuse is regularly neglected. Restricting get entry to to monetary sources, taking advantage of joint bills, prohibiting employment, or the use of coins as a shape of manipulation or punishment are all examples of this exercise. To understand the signs of economic abuse, one need to be aware about monetary restraints, superb financial manipulate, or coercive measures used to hold the sufferer financially based totally. Survivors must perceive times of monetary abuse to regain control over their autonomy and wreck a long way from the cycle of abuse they had been subjected to.

Chapter 2: The Cycle Of Abuse

The Cycle of Abuse dives into the problematic and regularly difficult pattern of abuse characteristic of many abusive relationships. This cycle can be determined in abusive relationships. It is essential to recognize this cycle to fully recognize the intricacies of abuse and the behaviors perpetuating it.

In this chapter, we are capable to speak the 3 levels of the abusive cycle: the building of hysteria, the outburst, and the reconciling of versions. The readers is probably capable of gain belief into the perpetuation of the cycle and discover avenues within the direction of breaking freed from it in the event that they deconstruct the dynamics at play for the duration of each step.

Phase 1: Tension-Building

The starting of the cycle is marked through the phase called "anxiety constructing," this is characterized thru a slow but ordinary increase in anxiety and soreness within the partnership. During this phase, conversation will become extra hard, and there may be an increase in minor arguments and misunderstandings. The sufferer frequently develops a hypervigilant u . S . In which they are trying to are anticipating the feelings of the abuser and seeks to hold the peace. As the tension rises, the victim also can discover themselves discounting their needs and tiptoeing across the abuser's triggers to keep away from scary the abuser's rage or aggressive behavior.

Increased complaint, passive-competitive behavior, withholding affection, or verbal and emotional outbursts from the abuser are all capacity signs of strain rising within the dating. A heightened revel in of tension, worry, and a loss of manage over one's very very very own existence are common feelings that patients of crime face. Because it prepares the manner for the subsequent explosive section, this section is important to apprehend the cycle sincerely.

Phase 2: Explosion

The forestall of the constructed-up strain in the relationship is the explosion segment, which results in a worrying and frequently violent incident for all activities worried. The eruption may additionally emerge in various workplace paintings, from verbal and emotional abuse to bodily violence. These are surely a number of the viable effects. The significance of the explosion may also moreover exchange relying on the person of the abusive dating that prompted it. The abuser vents their rage, expresses their dissatisfaction, and carrying sports activities their manage over the situation as an example in their power, which leaves the victim feeling helpless and terrified.

During the explosion section, sufferers are subjected to at the least one or extra of the subsequent kinds of mistreatment: extreme verbal abuse, excessive bodily violence, or sexual violence. In certain instances, sufferers experience all of these kinds of abuse concurrently. The sufferer's safety and well-being are mounted jeopardy, and they may hold physical injuries, emotional stress, and an excessive feeling of terror and powerlessness due to the attack. It is essential to recognize that the explosion segment is in no way the victim's fault; instead, it's far the stop result of the abuser's call for for energy and manage.

Phase 3: Reconciliation

After the explosion, the cycle actions into the reconciliation segment, marked through a period of peace and a temporary respite from the chaos that has been wrecked. The wrongdoer of the abuse can also show remorse, make an apology to the sufferer, and engage in acts of care and kindness toward them. They should make assurances that they might adjust their behavior and apologize, so deceiving the victim into believing that the abusive incident become an isolated occurrence and that there can be choice for the destiny in their courting.

During this degree, patients frequently experience feelings which might be hard to reconcile. They might also additionally have a ray of optimism, passionately yearning for the man or woman with whom they fell in love to return lower back decrease back to them in a permanent ability. When coupled with the dread of being abused yet again or the concern of abandonment, this desire can produce a powerful highbrow tie that makes it hard for sufferers to interrupt loose from the cycle of abuse.

Because it continues the sufferer emotionally committed to the relationship and hopes subjects will improve, the reconciliation segment plays a essential role within the staying electricity of abusive relationships. However, it's far essential to maintain in mind that the reconciliation section is extraordinary quick and that the cycle will always move again to the section of developing tension, ultimately principal to any other explosion.

Chapter 3: Psychological Manipulation

Abusers have get right of entry to to a effective device in the form of intellectual manipulation, which they use to gather manipulate over their victims, decline their revel in of self confidence, and preserve the cycle of abuse. This financial disaster investigates the numerous techniques and strategies abusers hire to govern their patients and erode their revel in of self esteem, identity, and employer. Readers can amplify interest, recognize the symptoms and signs and symptoms and signs, and get higher their electricity whilst the writer exposes misleading moves like the ones and sheds mild on them.

Gaslighting:

Gaslighting is a mental manipulation in which the wrongdoer casts doubt on the integrity in their aim's perceptions, recollections, and country of thoughts. The abuser did everything they'll to make the victim question and be bewildered approximately the region spherical them. Denying or trivializing the sufferer's reports, twisting information, or possibly developing incidents are all ability additives of the gaslighting technique. With time, the sufferer also can furthermore begin to query their very very very own sanity, coming to depend on the abuser's warped interpretation of the reality.

Because gaslighting is regularly diffused, it may be hard for sufferers to apprehend whilst they are being manipulated. The perpetrator of the abuse might also rent strategies which include trivializing the victim's emotions, transferring responsibility, or maybe projecting their very own behaviors onto the victim to justify their moves. This goals to set up an imbalance of power in which the victim turns into often reliant at the abuser for affirmation and a revel in of what's taking place inside the international.

Isolation:

Abusers have a terrific tool at their disposal that they employ to control and weaken their sufferers, and that device is putting aside their sufferers. The abuser makes it more difficult for the victim to are trying to find useful useful resource or mind-set from others through setting apart them from their social help networks or proscribing their get right of access to to the ones networks. This makes the victim more based totally. Isolation can take area progressively, with the abuser slowly discouraging or weakening the victim's relationships, or it is able to display up extra overtly, with strategies together with proscribing touch with buddies and own family or controlling the sufferer's actions and communique. Isolation can occur regularly, with the abuser subtly discouraging or undermining the sufferer's relationships, or it could take area greater openly.

The abuser also can create a story wherein the victim's pals and family are portrayed as volatile or untrustworthy to distort the victim's effect of others. The abuser continues a feature of electricity and manage over the sufferer via using maintaining aside the sufferer, which leaves the sufferer with the advent of being trapped and without any out of doors help networks.

Manipulative Mind Games:

To preserve manage over their sufferers, abusers frequently have interaction in an entire lot of thoughts video games which might be manipulative in nature. These thoughts games can contain strategies including pointing the finger at blame, giving the silent treatment, no longer expressing affection or being intimate, and always converting the ground guidelines or expectancies. The abuser continues the sufferer off-stability via way of normally converting the norms and expectations, resulting in instability and anxiety for the victim.

The abuser may also use the victim's guilt as a weapon through making them enjoy chargeable for his or her abusive conduct or with the aid of the use of emotional blackmail to coerce compliance. Another regular method is to withhold affection, verbal exchange, and emotional connection to exert manipulate over the abused person. This is known as the silent remedy. The sufferer's self-self notion suffers because of the abuser's manipulative mind video games, leaving them with emotions of inadequacy, unworthiness, and an first rate need to fulfill the abuser.

Emotional Manipulation:

Emotional manipulation is a important issue of intellectual abuse, which goals to exert manipulate over the victim's ideas, feelings, and behaviors. The abuser can also additionally moreover lease techniques like "love bombing," in which they lavish the sufferer with immoderate affection and hobby, best to later eliminate it to exert manage over them. Because of this, a cycle of rewards and punishments is created, which keeps the sufferer emotionally invested within the state of affairs and searching out validation and splendor from the abuser.

Other techniques of emotional manipulation include being relentlessly critical of the goal, humiliating them, transferring the responsibility onto a person else, and taking benefit of the sufferer's vulnerabilities and anxieties. These strategies can be hired with the aid of the abuser to preserve the victim off-balance, purpose the victim to impeach their very very own rate, and inspire the sufferer to rely on the abuser for validation and balance.

Chapter 4: Physical And Sexual Abuse

Abuse of any kind, whether or not or not or no longer it is physical or sexual, leaves victims with extreme wounds, both intellectual and physical, in addition to emotional and intellectual scars that might remaining a life-time. This chapter goals to create reputation, validate the reviews of survivors, and offer course on a manner to looking for safety, help, and recuperation. We discover the man or woman, consequences, and consequences of physical and sexual abuse.

Physical Abuse:

The use of physical stress or violence to exert manipulate over a victim and inflict ache on them is what is supposed with the resource of the usage of the time period "bodily abuse." It includes a considerable sort of sports activities, in conjunction with hitting, punching, slapping, kicking, choking, or any act that causes physical pain or damage to the sufferer. The intention of the abuser is to exercise dominance over the sufferer, activate fear in them, and hold themselves in a function of power over them.

Abuse of a physical kind may also moreover take the form of singular occurrences or exchange into a recurrent pattern in the context of the relationship. It is commonplace for the severity to boom through the years, leaving the man or woman with persistent fear and anxiety. To apprehend the symptoms of bodily abuse, one have to pay close interest to obvious injuries, bruising that doesn't have an evidence, fractures, or every different bodily markers. It is of the utmost importance to popularity on that the sufferer of physical abuse is in no way accountable and that trying to find assistance is an critical step closer to each safety and recuperation.

Sexual Abuse:

Sexual abuse is a form of mistreatment that may cause immoderate mental trauma because it includes sexual acts closer to the sufferer's will, coercion, or exploitation. It consists of a extensive spectrum of actions, which embody rape, forced sexual acts, unwanted contact, verbal or emotional manipulation for sexual reasons, or any sexual hobby wherein an unwilling person is coerced into taking detail. The sufferer's physical autonomy, dignity, and sense of self are all violated whilst they will be patients of sexual abuse.

It may be hard to understand the signs and symptoms of sexual attack because survivors of such abuse occasionally enjoy disgrace, remorse, and confusion about their reviews. Symptoms also can consist of physical accidents in intimate areas, rapid shifts in behavior or mood, tension or aversion inside the route of sexual activities, or discomfort at the equal time as discussing non-public subjects. It is important to offer a putting this is steady and loose from judgment for survivors with the intention to communicate about their research, look for resource, and discover assets to assist them heal.

Impact and Consequences:

Abuse, whether or not physical or sexual, has repercussions which may be a long way-conducting and extend properly past the intense physical damage carried out. The impact is physical and mental, leaving survivors with immoderate intellectual misery and a protracted-lasting have an effect on on their physical fitness.

The abuse sufferer may moreover be afflicted by accidents, damaged bones, bruises, wounds, or various other bodily illnesses as an instantaneous end end result of the abuse. These wounds almost continuously necessitate clinical treatment, and they will have extended-time period repercussions for the sufferer's bodily properly-being and the whole first-rate of lifestyles. As a similarly effect of the abuse they were subjected to, survivors may also face lengthy-term pain, limited mobility, and lots of distinct bodily ailments.

Abuse of any kind, whether physical or sexual, can also have devastating effects on a person's intellectual health. Survivors can also moreover experience signs and symptoms of placed up-disturbing stress disorder (PTSD), sadness, tension, disordered ingesting, self-inflicted harm, or mind of suicide. They might in all likelihood be stricken by way of a excessive loss of recollect, have problem growing healthful relationships, and function a warped view of the manner masses they will be precious to themselves. The demanding revel in of abuse can permeate all facets of a survivor's existence, affecting their intellectual health, potential to have interaction with others, and a stylish sense of safety.

Seeking Safety and Support:

It is of the most significance for survivors of bodily and sexual abuse to are in search of for a stable haven and get help. It is essential for parents which are going thru the experience of abuse to apprehend that they are no longer by myself and that help is on hand to them.

Developing a protection plan is vital for survivors on the point of flee or break out a risky situation. This may imply contacting community domestic abuse hotlines, looking for sanctuary in stable homes, or confiding in trusted friends, own family individuals, or professionals who can offer help and route. Taking criminal movement, which include filing for a restraining order or pursuing some extraordinary shape of felony recourse, also can be crucial to securing one's protection.

Chapter 5: Emotional And Verbal Abuse

Within violent relationships, emotional and verbal abuse digs into the extreme and lengthy-lasting effect of emotional and verbal abuse on someone. Even despite the fact that the ones types of mistreatment won't leave visible scars, the intellectual traumas they inflict may be sincerely as immoderate, if not extra so, than the physical scars they depart within the once more of.

This financial ruin dreams to increase awareness, validate the critiques of survivors, and offer assist for recuperation, rebuilding vanity, and reclaiming personal energy. We study emotional and verbal abuse's nature, strategies, and impact.

Emotional Abuse:

Abuse on an emotional degree is characterised with the useful resource of the usage of the sluggish destruction of a person's experience of vanity, self confidence, and emotional well-being. The abuser earnings control over the victim thru conducting abusive behaviors closer to them, inclusive of relentless criticism, consistent manipulation, degradation, and humiliation. In evaluation to physical abuse, emotional abuse can go away unseen scars, making it hard to emerge as privy to the damage to a person's intellectual fitness but have vast repercussions for his or her lives.

Belittling the victim regularly, calling them nasty names, insulting them, and the usage of language purported to denigrate and devalue them are all examples of techniques that may be implemented in emotional abuse. The abuser may additionally moreover lower the sufferer's accomplishments, lessen them off from their assist networks, or purpose them emotional ache. The sufferer of emotional abuse evaluations emotions of entrapment and helplessness due to the environment of dread, tension, and dependency created by the usage of the usage of the abuser.

Verbal Abuse:

The use of terms with the reason to motive the victim bodily ache, intellectual suffering, or social humiliation constitutes a shape of mistreatment called verbal abuse. It can manifest itself in various techniques, which include yelling and shouting, making threats, and making insulting feedback. The reason of controlling, intimidating, and silencing the sufferer thru verbal abuse is to go away the sufferer feeling helpless and voiceless.

The culprit of the abuse may additionally furthermore use phrases to control, blame, or shame the victim, undermining their self-self guarantee and warping their perception of the location spherical them. Verbal abuse may be harsh and continual, taking area in non-public or public settings and humiliating the sufferer inside the the front of others on motive. Verbal abuse has a profoundly awful have an impact on, one that may bring about emotions of embarrassment, guilt, and uncertainty approximately one's very very own skills.

Gaslighting and Psychological Manipulation:

Gaslighting and other forms of intellectual manipulation are not unusual components of verbal and emotional abuse, and they serve to exacerbate the victim's pain and feel of disorientation. A individual may be gaslighted whilst subjected to manipulation that calls into doubt the sufferer's perceptions, memories, and sanity. The abuser manipulates the victim's notion of reality with the useful useful resource of distorting the reality, denying or brushing off their evaluations, and trivializing their importance.

Gaslighting can take the shape of the abuser rejecting unstable acts, transferring responsibility onto the sufferer, or maybe growing sports to steer the sufferer's view of fact. It moreover may be the abuser blaming the victim for the abuse. Because of this deliberate manipulation, the sufferer begins offevolved to question their judgment, reminiscence, and sanity, further eroding their functionality to just accept as genuine with themselves. The sufferer may want to probably have the effect that they're dropping their maintain on truth, and they might end up increasingly relying at the abuser for validation and a sense of safety.

Long-Term Impact:

The poor consequences of verbal and emotional abuse should have severe and a ways-accomplishing repercussions in the end. Victims frequently go through a devastating blow to their self-esteem, self confidence, and self notion. They can acquire symptoms of anxiety, sadness, complex publish-stressful strain disorder (C-PTSD), and certainly one of a kind psychiatric ailments.

Those who've survived physical, sexual, or verbal abuse are more likely to battle self-doubt, have problem constructing awesome relationships, and find it difficult to set healthy limitations. Because they were continuously invalidated and devalued, it is able to be hard for them to remember their very own emotions and judgment, and they may be greater vulnerable to self-blame and self-complaint because of their stories.

Healing and Reclaiming Personal Power:

Recovering from the damage because of verbal and emotional abuse is a journey that calls for persistence, aid, and self-compassion. Seeking out remedy and counseling from specialists specializing in trauma and abuse can offer abuse survivors the property to technique their reviews, get higher their arrogance, and create healthy coping strategies. These gear may be acquired thru remedy and counseling.

For survivors, participation in aid organizations and corporations made from pals can offer validation, statistics, and a experience of belonging. Participating in sports activities selling nicely-being, together with schooling mindfulness, retaining a journal, carrying out modern expression, or getting normal exercise, also can speed up restoration.

Chapter 6: Financial Abuse

Abuse wherein the abuser exerts manipulate over the victim via using manipulating the victim's get right of entry to to and manage over cash assets is called financial abuse. This bankruptcy intends to shed light on economic abuse's nature, techniques, and repercussions, providing survivors with the know-how and belongings crucial to interrupt unfastened from this mistreatment and restore their economic independence. This financial disaster furthermore goals to provide survivors with the information and assets to interrupt unfastened from this injustice and reclaim their monetary freedom.

Understanding Financial Abuse:

Abusers will motel to numerous strategies, collectively with economic abuse, to accumulate strength and have an effect on over the ones they abuse. It includes workout manipulate over the victim's economic scenario, preventing the victim from getting access to cash, and employing monetary resources as a tool for manipulation and punishment. The abuser restricts the victim's ability to make selections independently and to hold their autonomy once they have manipulate over their victim's monetary assets.

Tactics of Financial Abuse:

Abuse of one's financial characteristic can take many splendid paperwork. The abuser may additionally moreover purposefully reduce off the victim's get entry to to employment or instructional possibilities, causing the sufferer to turn out to be economically dependent on the abuser for his or her fundamental need. They may additionally additionally have whole manipulate over the sufferer's financial topics, manipulate their financial institution debts, and restriction their get right of access to to cash, credit score score gambling playing cards, and unique monetary documents. The perpetrator of the abuse may also sabotage the sufferer's expert existence with the aid of inflicting interruptions at artwork, stopping the victim from attending artwork, or undermining profession possibilities. They might probably run up money owed within the sufferer's name, making the victim chargeable for duties that they did not create for themselves financially. In addition, the abuser might also moreover need to cover statistics approximately the circle of relatives's monetary feature, making it tough for the sufferer to recognize and manage their monetary situation. They may additionally additionally confiscate and sell the victim's belongings without their permission, decreasing off their get entry to to some thing belongings or resources they'll have.

Consequences of Financial Abuse:

Abuse within the form of cash may additionally moreover have devastating effects on someone's physical and highbrow health, similarly to their potential to go away an abusive dating. It regularly leaves sufferers financially unstable, making it hard to find out housing, meet their simple necessities, or enlarge economic independence. It can be difficult for patients to are searching for prison resource, acquire counseling, or get proper of get entry to to aid programs because of the fact they'll have limited get entry to to cash, credit score rating, or one-of-a-type financial property. The victim is extra depending on the abuser because of the abuser's use of price range, making it more hard for the victim to go away the relationship and preserve their agency. The abuser's sports, which incorporates gathering debt within the sufferer's name or defaulting on financial responsibilities, will have lengthy-lasting repercussions, which can also bring about the victim's credit score being broken due to the abuse.

Breaking Free and Reclaiming Financial Independence:

Getting out of an abusive monetary scenario wishes cautious planning and help. The following are some of the steps that survivors can take to reclaim their economic independence:

1. Educate Yourself: Learn approximately monetary literacy, collectively with developing a budget, recognizing your rights and options, and handling credit score.

2. Secure Important Documents: Collect vital files, which include identification, financial records, and criminal documents, and preserve them in a strong place this is out of the abuser's draw close to.

three. Create a Safety Net: Establish a separate monetary group account whenever it's far viable to keep cash and assemble a financial safety net.

4. Seek Professional Help: Seek the advice of a monetary consultant, felony professional, or domestic violence advocate who can offer path on monetary subjects and criminal options.

Chapter 7: Breaking The Silence

The first step inside the course of healing, locating help, and reclaiming one's voice and enterprise business agency is to interrupt the silence, an empowering act. In this economic ruin, we've a look at why survivors usually live mute, the effect of silence on their properly-being, and techniques to interrupt loose from the shackles of silence. These are all topics which are blanketed on this bankruptcy. We desire that by using throwing moderate in this crucial adventure, we're in a position on the way to validate the testimonies of survivors, foster open discourse, and empower people to inform their recollections.

The Power of Silence:

The memories of humans who have survived violent relationships are often shrouded in silence. Fear, shame, guilt, societal stigma, and the abuser's manipulations are only some of the variables that play a function in retaining sufferers silent. The reasons for silence are many and complex. Survivors could be afraid of being blamed, disbelieved, or retaliated toward. They should have emotions of disgrace or believe they will be responsible for the abuse in some manner. It may be difficult for survivors of abusive relationships to talk up and get treatment because of the social stigma surrounding abusive relationships and the associated myths.

The Impact of Silence:

The lack of debate of violent relationships have to have large and terrible outcomes at the well-being of these who have survived such relationships. It reinforces emotions of loneliness, humiliation, and guilt directed toward oneself. The abuser is predicated upon on the sufferer's silence to maintain control and strength over them. Hence the abuse can satisfactory preserve if the sufferer remains silent. A decline in highbrow fitness, in conjunction with signs and symptoms and symptoms of disappointment, anxiety, placed up-worrying strain illness (PTSD), and mind of hopelessness, would possibly probably result from internalizing the quiet and maintaining it to oneself.

Breaking the Silence:

It takes bravery and freedom to interrupt the silence. Yet, it represents the begin of a way which can motive healing and transformation. The selection need to be made on a person-via-person basis, at the survivor's private tempo, and regular with their private values. When it includes breaking the quiet, the subsequent are a few strategies to recollect:

Self-Reflection and Acceptance: Recognize that you are not by myself and that the abuse emerge as now not your fault. Also, understand which you aren't the most effective who triggered it. Adopt an attitude of self-compassion and well known that telling your story is a vital step toward healing.

Identify Trusted Support Systems: Determine the people to your life with whom you have got got whole self assurance and might talk overtly approximately a few aspect. This might also moreover encompass humans you understand out of your social circle, members of your circle of relatives, therapists, or help organizations. During this sensitive time, surrounding oneself with others who are empathic and understand what you are going thru can offer the important guide.

Consult an Expert If You Need Help: You could probably want to the touch therapists, counselors, or advocates who art work with those who have survived abuse. They can offer route, validation, and help as you're making your manner thru breaking the silence.

Educate Yourself: Get your self informed at the mechanics of abuse, your rights, and the assets which are accessible to you. Learning about the dynamics of abusive relationships let you advantage a feel of enterprise enterprise and will let you make greater nicely-informed selections about whether or no longer or no longer or now not to speak up.

Express Yourself: Find strategies to precise your self which are considerable to you and pursue them. This may additionally moreover furthermore contain writing in a journal, generating art work or song, conducting musical sports activities, and turning into a member of manual groups in which you may talk your reviews and feelings with others who have been via conditions similar to yours.

Advocate for Change: Think about advocating for people who have conquer abuse. You may additionally help damage the silence on a much wider scale via spreading interest, thinking cultural attitudes, and supporting corporations operating to stop abuse.

By gaining an interest of the factors that make contributions to silence, its consequences on survivors, and the methods that can be used to interrupt free from it, we're hoping to allow people to reclaim their voices, search for assist, and talk approximately their stories.

Chapter 8: Leaving An Abusive Relationship

Leaving an abusive relationship is a brave desire that takes careful making plans, aid, and a willingness to position one's protection and nicely-being on the pinnacle of one's priorities. In this financial disaster, we dig into the issues that make leaving difficult, the importance of safety planning, and the techniques that can be completed to conquer the emotional, logistical, and criminal problems that can stand up. Our reason is to offer human beings with the knowledge and gear they need to take the important steps closer to a life loose from abuse through offering in-depth facts and property.

Understanding the Challenges of Leaving:

Getting a ways from an abusive associate isn't regularly a truthful gadget. There are many incredible troubles that survivors need to face, together with the subsequent:

1.   Fear for Safety: If the abused individual attempts to go away, the abuser might also

have threatened them with bodily damage, stalking, or reprisal. There is a great quantity of scenario spherical the fear of 1's private safety and the safety of one's children or extraordinary dependents.

2. Emotional Bond: Those who've survived abuse may additionally moreover revel in a number of conflicting emotions for their abuser, including emotions of love, attachment, or dependency. Severing this emotional tie may be fraught with peril and problem.

3. Economic Dependence: It may be difficult for survivors to turn out to be financially independent or to provide for themselves and their youngsters if they may be economically depending on their abuser due to the abuser's use of economic abuse and control.

4. Isolation: Abusers often reduce off their patients' get proper of access to to help structures, leaving them with fewer property and plenty much less social connections than they might in any other case have.

5.   Societal Stigma and Shame: Survivors can fear that others will determine them, blame them, or not believe them, which can save you them from getting assist or exposing the abuse.

Safety Planning:

The steering of a protection plan is an vital step inside the method of leaving an abusive dating. It entails growing an individualized technique to shield the survivor's protection and the safety of any dependents they may have.

Navigating the Legal Process:

1.   Leaving an abusive relationship may need to mean going thru the prison system to make sure your protection and protection. The following are a few legal considerations:

2.   Restraining Orders and Protection Orders: Consult with jail professionals to discover the potential of acquiring a restraining order or safety order in competition to the abuser,

that could legally ban them from contacting or coming close to you.

3. Child Custody and Support: If kids are worried, you have to get crook advice regarding custody preparations and little one manual duties to protect their first-rate hobbies and offer for them.

four. Divorce and Property Settlements: If you're married or live in a cohabiting courting, you have to searching out the advice of an felony expert to advantage an know-how of the manner for getting a divorce or a separation and to keep your rights regarding assets, assets, and economic useful resource.

five. Document Incidents: Maintain a log of the times of abuse which have taken vicinity, noting the dates, an outline of every incident, similarly to any evidence on the side of photos or messages. This fabric can also show to be essential in the direction of judicial movements.

Emotional Support and Healing:

Getting out of a dating wherein one is being abused is essential to recuperation and rebuilding one's existence. Putting your self first and carrying out out to others for emotional manual is crucial. Take underneath consideration the following:

1.   Therapeutic Support: Participate in character psychotherapy or counseling to paintings thru the annoying experience, repair your self confidence, and installation powerful coping strategies.

2.   Support Groups: Joining a survivor network or a manual business enterprise can allow you to hook up with humans who've been through a few element just like what you've got got been thru, share your studies, and accumulate validation and guide.

three.   Self-Care Practices: Exercise, practising mindfulness, maintaining a magazine, task pastimes, and pursuing contemporary stores are examples of self-care activities that promote recovery and properly-being. Practice these objects often.

4.   Establish Boundaries: Establish secure obstacles with the person that abused you and others. Put your very very very own health and safety first, and do no longer be afraid to face your ground concerning the limits you've got set.

5.   Seek Financial and Legal Assistance: It is on your pleasant hobby to are looking for the advice of criminal and economic experts to understand your rights, responsibilities, and the property at your disposal. They will guide you thru the approach and shield your financial balance.

Chapter 9: Rebuilding And Healing

After enduring the demanding effects of abuse, one will need time, staying strength, and self-compassion to rebuild one's lifestyles. This bankruptcy delves into the severa factors of the technique of rebuilding, together with emotional healing, self-discovery, regaining independence, and developing wholesome relationships which is probably involved. Our challenge is to equip survivors with the device vital for restoration, resiliency, and private improvement by using imparting them with precise statistics and actionable techniques.

Emotional Healing:

Rebuilding one's existence after being abused requires emotional recovery as a primary popularity. Acknowledging and running with the intellectual and emotional scars of the abusive relationship is vital for this device. A stable and supportive surroundings may be created for survivors to discover their feelings, locate recuperation from the beyond, and broaden wholesome coping capabilities with the resource of manner of having them participate in treatment or counseling with expert professionals working with trauma and abuse.

Healing may be fostered through the usage of strategies for emotional law. These strategies embody deep respiratory sports activities, mindfulness meditation, journaling, and taking component in creative expression. Self-reflected photograph and self-compassion are critical components of interest of one's emotions, wishes, and beliefs. It is feasible to lessen the emotional toll that demanding memories have on a person and boost up the recuperation approach via the use of on foot with a therapist to way and reframe such recollections.

Self-Discovery and the Reclaiming of Identity:

Rebuilding one's existence after being abused calls for one to rediscover and repair their experience of identity. Survivors can pursue pursuits and sports activities sports that cause them to happy and assist them connect with their genuine selves. Survivors can define their course and feature amusing each milestone they attain if they devise non-public desires and aspirations in severa elements in their lives, along with their careers, educations, relationships, and private improvement.

It is possible to growth one's self-esteem and nurture self-assure via cultivating self-self guarantee via notable self-communicate, self-affirmations, and thankfulness. When prioritizing one's properly-being and enhancing one's authority, placing boundaries and nicely articulating one's desires and expectancies is vital.

Reclaiming Independence:

Regaining one's revel in of autonomy is important to the healing method following abuse. The pursuit of employment, the crowning glory of education or training, and the exercising of responsible cash manipulate are all techniques wherein survivors can also moreover float in the course of reaching financial autonomy.

It is vital to domesticate supportive networks of pals, own family, and experts who can provide path, encouragement, and resource in a practical experience. These networks need to be developed. Taking benefit of private growth and improvement possibilities, which includes attending workshops, taking detail in beneficial useful resource companies, or undertaking sports activities activities that foster self-development, can in addition empower survivors. Contributing to recovering one's independence is broadening one's social ties and forming new relationships that align with one's values and foster a healthy and uplifting environment.

Chapter 10: Breaking The Cycle

Understanding the styles and dynamics that make contributions to abusive behaviors, addressing the underlying motives, and actively on foot toward growing wholesome and respectful relationships are all critical steps in breaking the cycle and ending it. This monetary disaster discusses the motives for the cycle's persevered life, strategies for escaping terrible behaviors, and the importance of private development and duty. We want to empower individuals to interrupt some distance from the cycle of abuse and create a destiny complete of healthful and correct connections with the aid of offering them with in-depth data and guidance this is each practical and applicable.

Understanding the Cycle of Abuse:

The sample of abuse, moreover known as the cycle of abuse, is a pattern that is repeated in lots of abusive relationships. It regularly contains three tiers: the duration wherein anxiety is built up, the phase in which there's each explosive or abusive conduct, and the phase in which there is either honeymooning or reconciliation. Understanding this cycle is essential to interrupt free from its maintain. Survivors regularly find out themselves not in a position to interrupt out from the cycle of abuse because of the reality they mistakenly experience that they have got the strength to adjust the abusive associate's behavior or desire that the honeymoon section will closing all the time. The first step toward breaking a cycle is recognizing that the cycle exists.

Breaking Free from the Cycle:

A multi-pronged approach that emphasizes personal improvement, introspection, and abilties improvement for healthful relationships is wanted to break the sample of abusive relationships. One of the techniques that can be used to interrupt loose from an abusive relationship is to educate oneself approximately the man or woman of abusive relationships, strength and manage, and properly dating styles. Engaging in a few form of self-meditated photograph is crucial to understand one's very personal patterns and movements in relationships and any previous demanding research or unresolved problems that is a component in awful dynamics.

When it comes to partnerships, it's miles vital to efficiently communicate one's needs, expectancies, and boundaries with one's partner and installation clear and robust obstacles within the ones interactions. Seeking out a therapist or counselor expert to deal with underlying troubles and educate healthy relationship abilities can offer useful guidance, manual, and tools for finishing the cycle of dangerous conduct. Developing proper coping mechanisms, which encompass nice verbal exchange, self-care sports activities, and techniques for emotional regulation, is also a essential part of the way.

It is essential to surround oneself with a useful resource machine consisting of reliable people, together with friends, own family people, or help group people, to receive encouragement, statistics, and validation. When humans take duty for his or her acts and determine to personal development, they damage the cycle made feasible through the use of obligation and personal increase gambling crucial roles. It is likewise vital to address inclinations in the direction of codependence and to develop healthy interdependence to stop the cycle.

By breaking the silence and discussing one's critiques and observations with different humans, you can help growth cognizance about abusive relationships, useful resource other survivors, and art work towards breaking the cycle on a societal diploma. Individuals can destroy loose from abusive behaviors and create a future for themselves this is complete of respect, empathy, and healthy connections if they do the steps stated here.

Chapter 11: Supporting Loved Ones

It is critical to offer those whose lives had been impacted thru abuse with compassion, empathy, and resource in a sensible feel. This financial disaster discusses diverse methods people can offer assist, emphasizing active listening, promoting restoration, and the empowerment of survivors. The reader will collect the equipment crucial to be a supply of electricity and help for his or her cherished ones due to the thorough information and practical help supplied in this text.

Understanding the Impact:

These connections profoundly effect the survivors of abusive relationships and people who care about them. It is important that the affects of abuse, which could encompass physical, emotional, and mental trauma, low conceitedness, anxiety, sadness, and feelings of isolation, be stated. The provision of suitable guide calls for, first and critical, an information of the multifaceted nature of abuse further to the outcomes of abuse.

Active Listening and Validation:

Listening to and validating the reports of these you care about is one of the maximum beneficial strategies to offer assist. Ensure they have got a place where they may not be judged or interrupted at the identical time as sharing their thoughts, emotions, and stories without fear of reprisal. Pay near interest to what they have got to say, validate their feelings, and reassure them in their price and electricity. The maximum vital aspect is to offer empathic and nonjudgmental assist while heading off giving unsolicited recommendation or downplaying their research.

Empowerment and Encouragement:

When you assist loved ones, imparting them the tools and encouragement they want to begin restoration and reclaiming their lives is important. Encourage and remind them of the characteristics that lead them to robust and resilient. Assist them in locating and gaining access to numerous options, which includes remedy, resource groups, jail useful resource, and exclusive expert assistance. Encourage them to make choices that positioned their health and properly-being first and provide them possibilities for personal development and deal with themselves.

Safety Planning:

When supplying useful aid to loved ones who're in abusive conditions, protection preparation is virtually crucial. Assist them in formulating a custom designed protection plan that facts the moves they're able to take to protect themselves and any dependents they will have. This may additionally furthermore entail locating strong areas, defensive important papers, choosing a sign or code word to apply within the occasion of drawing near threat, and formulating a plan for effective communique. Encourage them to contact nearby assist corporations or helplines that specialize in supporting abuse survivors in their vicinity.

Educate Yourself:

Educating your self on abusive relationships, the dynamics of strength and manage, and the available resources to effectively useful useful resource the victim of abuse is crucial. Educate your self at the signs and symptoms and symptoms of abuse, its outcomes on survivors, and the stressful conditions they may face even as looking for help. Maintaining recognition of neighborhood rules, assist services, and helplines that can be useful inside the help device may be sincerely useful. When the nuances of abuse are understood, help can be supplied that is higher informed and additional specially directed.

Self-Care for Supporters:

It can be specially taxing to assist loved ones in coping with the aftereffects of abuse. Make searching after yourself a top priority to defend your fitness and maintain your viability as a deliver of assist. Find a way to guide yourself, whether or not through the assist of buddies, own family, guide groups, or maybe treatment. Establish suitable barriers to defend yourself from burnout, and make sure to time table time to your time desk for activities that offer you delight and rest. Remember that searching after your self is crucial to provide real resource.

Allies can offer crucial energy and guide in the occasion that they understand the effect of abuse, have interaction in lively listening, empower survivors, useful beneficial useful resource with protection planning, educate themselves, and prioritize self-care. Their factor in helping their cherished ones on their route to recuperation and empowerment is vital to the challenge's fulfillment.

Chapter 12: Advocacy And Empowerment

To respond to and save you abuse, advocacy includes developing recognition, thinking societal norms, and promoting systemic change. The purpose of empowering survivors is to offer them with the records, tools, and property important for them to reclaim control in their lives and make alternatives which is probably in their brilliant interests.

This financial disaster investigates the various sides of advocacy and empowerment, which includes individual and collective efforts, legal options, network help, and the significance of cultivating a subculture of empathy and duty. To empower readers to come to be champions and dealers of alternate inside the warfare toward abusive relationships, we will provide readers with in-intensity records and help at the way to located that records into exercising.

Understanding Advocacy:

Advocacy is the act of speaking up on behalf of, presenting assist to, and defensive the rights and properly-being of ladies and men who have been abused. It entails wondering cultural attitudes contributing to the continuation of violence, demanding obligation from establishments, and pushing regulations protective survivors. Advocacy can tackle various office work, from individual movements to collective efforts, and it plays an crucial detail in putting in a tradition that condemns abusive behaviors and seeks to rectify them.

Individual Advocacy:

The first step in man or woman advocacy is helping survivors of their quest for recuperation and justice and giving them the business enterprise to make their private options. Providing emotional assist, supporting survivors plan for their safety, and connecting them with the critical belongings and services are all examples of what this consists of. Individual advocates can assist survivors in navigating prison methods, accompany them to courtroom hearings or appointments, and offer data about the rights they'll be entitled to. Individual advocates make a contribution to survivors' empowerment and guide their conviction of their very very own price and organization enterprise organisation through status along the survivors.

Collective Advocacy:

Advocating on behalf of a cause together is joining forces with extremely good people and organizations that percent the same desires to result in extra exchange. It includes sports activities at the grassroots level, network organizing, and collaborative projects to growth public attention about abusive relationships, train the overall public, and advise for law improvements. Collective advocates make a contribution to the removal of the mechanisms that permit abuse and the selling of a society this is extra supportive and equitable thru sports along side the corporation of events, participation in public campaigns, and engagement with legislators.

Legal Advocacy:

Advocacy in the criminal sphere centers on the use of the judicial device to defend and assist survivors. Legal advocates collaborate intently with survivors to provide advice on to be had crook choices, offer an cause for prison rights and processes, and advocate on survivors' behalf within the jail device. They is probably in a function to help you get restraining orders, guide you via custody disputes, and are looking for justice through criminal or civil actions. Advocates for victims' rights are essential in allowing abuse victims to stand up for his or her legal entitlements and demand duty for the wrongs they've got suffered.

Chapter 13: Understanding The Landscape Of

Nuclear Narcissism

We surprise why we start relationships that seem so acquainted to us from the very beginning. The people that we've got hobby in frequently encompass a familiar profile or script. When upon first assembly them, they appear appealing, captivating, realistic, and are full of electricity and notable stories, often approximately themselves, their lives, and what they're doing, but all of the on the identical time as showing little to no interest about us or our nicely-being. But despite the fact that, we're fascinated and rapid ensnared. We are thru hook or via manner of crook interested in them. We are seduced into their emotional and mental internet and their global of "it is all about me."

Have you ever heard the expression, "You basically married your father or your mom"? Not in the physical sense, of route, however in the familiar behavioral styles that we grew up with and understand, taking in all the top similarly to the awful. For those individuals who had a narcissistic decide or in every mother and father, this is regularly the adorable reality. We recognise the dance of manipulation because we have been there earlier than as children growing up and witnessing it firsthand.

We are the harmless obedient participants for the duration of our growing years and regularly in our observations from our early beginnings, an amazing way to characteristic and carry out inside the dysfunctional fabric of our own family relational dynamics as we form and as we watch our lives spread in advance than us. We had been raised in this manner, as there have been no different alternatives wherein we had been allowed to perform. The own family area that we participated in covered toxic verbal exchange and behaviors that we found from the very people of our circle of relatives which have been supposed to have loved and guarded us.

So, while we meet someone in our adult lives that has acquainted developments and trends of our very own dad and mom or households, we experience right away comfortable, as though we've were given mentioned them for many years regardless of any purple flags that would floor whilst we meet them. We persuade ourselves to short push the flags aside. We succumb to them like moths to a slight at night time time time, in no manner in reality knowledge or predicting that sooner or later our wings receives burned and in the long run, both fly speedy away from the moderate to stay to tell the story or dangle to the extreme hot mild, unable to escape and in the end, perish.

It is significantly important to discover that to transport right away to a healthful relationship we want to harm down those acquainted lousy behavior and patterns that we as fast as so in detail knew and felt comfortable with and go away they all in the back of us so you can pass in advance to finding a genuinely healthful, loving dating that we're able to develop with and be satisfied.

It is exciting, however, that even though we'd inherently apprehend that there can be some element wrong with a courting this is entire of narcissistic behaviors that we're in, we regularly will maintain to defend this very relationship, as those had been the alternatives we made on the time that we met them and to renowned that we have been incorrect in our desire of a mate is to start with scarier than leaving a specifically poor narcissistic relationship this is doomed for failure.

So, What Is a Narcissist?

Narcissism is a persona contamination, and the entirety rotates round one character, the narcissist. This mental term originated from the Greek mythological character Narcissus, who fell in love along collectively together with his non-public contemplated picture.

In Greek mythology, the tale of Narcissus serves as a effective allegory for the concept of narcissism. According to the parable, Narcissus changed into a younger and surprisingly handsome hunter. He possessed an ethereal enchantment that captivated everybody round him. But his right downfall lay not in his bodily look, however in his loss of functionality to peer beyond himself.

 As the story is going, sooner or later, at the identical time as wandering thru the woods, Narcissus encountered a crystal-clean pool of water. As he slowly leaned over to take a drink from the pool of water, he caught a glimpse of his very non-public mirrored photo. Completely mesmerized via his very own beauty, Narcissus have grow to be right away infatuated collectively along with his non-public photograph, staring decrease again at himself. He couldn't tear his gaze faraway from his mirrored image, sincerely entranced via the magical appeal of his non-public mirrored image.

From that 2nd in advance, self-love fed on Narcissus. He spent hours on prevent with the aid of the water's factor, pining for the now not possible and ignoring the outside global and the affection of others; he have grow to be fixated mostly on himself. This infatuation grew into his obsession and his selflove of himself over a few thing else in his lifestyles.

Narcissus's story serves as a cautionary tale, highlighting the dangers of excessive self-obsession and self-admiration. It exemplifies how an person's fixation on their personal photograph and dreams can bring about a profound disconnection from reality and their surrounding humans. It well-knownshows the inherent tragedy that comes with completely valuing oneself, neglecting the dreams and emotions of others and normally completing in depressing, sad, failed relationships.

The fable of Narcissus gives a symbolic basis for expertise the roots and effects of narcissistic behavior. It reminds us of the significance of stability, empathy, and right human connectivity, reminding us to look beyond our very very very own reflections and recognize the beauty and properly properly well worth in those spherical us and the place beyond ourselves.

Narcissism in its conventional form is diagnosed as a man or woman trait or sickness characterised thru an excessive preoccupation with oneself, a grandiose experience of self-importance, and a lack of empathy for others, just like the Greek hunter, Narcissus.

Narcissism is a mental kingdom or person trait that manifests as extreme self-absorption, self-centeredness, and an inflated revel in of one's very very personal significance. Individuals with narcissistic tendencies display off a sturdy want for admiration, a enjoy of entitlement, and a dishonest to take advantage of others for personal gain.

Narcissism could have an impact on every non-public relationships and broader social dynamics. Characters or people with narcissistic tendencies constantly are searching for hobby, admiration, and validation from others, regularly brushing off the emotions and needs of these around them. They have an exaggerated revel in of their very own achievements, capabilities, and abilities, believing themselves to be superior to all others.

Case Study: "David," a Textbook Narcissist

Alicia had normally been a people pleaser. Growing up, she end up the middle little one that had come from a huge circle of relatives, and he or she had discovered out to hold the peace with the aid of going together with what really without a doubt absolutely everyone else wanted. She frequently may also surrender what she desired truly to help preserve the peace within the own family so there is probably a great deal less arguments among them. So as an adult, it changed into herbal that she might also supply this same trait into her marriage to someone named David.

David come to be good-looking, charming, and especially assured, but he had a dark factor that Alicia did not see in him initially till an awful lot later after they were married. He turned into a narcissist who manipulated and controlled Alicia, slowly but methodically chipping away at her conceitedness and independence over a few years.

In earlier years, Alicia did no longer recognize what have become taking region. She grow to be happy to do something David preferred, to make him happy and avoid any conflict, as struggle for Alicia become uncomfortable, however she grew to recognize over time David's intolerance for whatever that did no longer pass definitely his manner. As time went on, she started out to recognise that she had out of vicinity herself in the device of constantly searching for to make it okay for David in addition to for his or her relationship. She had no pals outside of her marriage, no pursuits or pursuits, and no enjoy of who she come to be aside from David. It turn out to be as though they had been joined at the hip and acted and reacted as one.

The turning factor in her existence came one midnight while David had a meltdown and raged at her over something very minor. Alicia had cooked dinner for him, however he complained that it became no longer suitable sufficient and threw the plate complete of food easy in the course of the room onto the wall, virtually lacking her head. Alicia changed into right now stunned and worrying, and she or he realized that his behavior had end up out of manage.

Over the following few weeks, Alicia began out to do a little studies on why David modified into acting within the way he changed into, and he or she quick got here throughout what narcissism and codependency have become. She observed that the want to delight others and avoid struggle modified into what she end up doing with David. She started to recognize that it made her liable to David's manipulation and manipulate over the numerous years they spent collectively. She herself commenced to find out that she had inadvertently helped to permit his conduct with out ever placing up any barriers or effects for him. But she additionally found out that it have turn out to be possible to interrupt free from this toxic dance that that they had with every different and recover from the connection that had enveloped her life for goodbye.

The first step for Alicia became to investigate what the relationship have end up and start to set boundaries with David. She counseled him that his behavior was now not appropriate and that she may not tolerate it. David have become initially irritated and defensive and attempted to first located all of the blame on her for him getting out of control. But Alicia stood agency. She refused to interact in his arguments or permit him control her alongside along with his superficial apologies or attraction her even as his arguments or bullying did now not art work.

As Alicia asserted herself together with her husband, she additionally rebuilt her revel in of self. She commenced out seeing a therapist who specialized in codependency and narcissistic abuse. She joined a assist company for people who've been thru similar research. She moreover started out out taking yoga training and rediscovered her love of painting. She commenced to take day journey for herself and for the topics that she had constantly preferred to do in her existence however by no means felt like she can also need to through the years, as David had woven a terrific net of isolation for her.

The method changed into relatively gradual and tough, but Alicia changed into determined to stay on. She started out out to look small changes in herself and of their relationship. She grow to be now not tolerating his outrageous conduct, and David slowly started to understand that he need to not control or control her, which persisted to infuriate him. Alicia moreover started out to see him for who he truely changed into, in preference to the idealized model of him that she had created in her mind of who he modified into, the captivating, good-looking, rushing man that she as quickly as met many years within the past. She turn out to be willing to meet all his flaws head-on. She turned into no longer glossing over any of them. She started out to look and understand that David became not able to have any perception to himself or to their relationship.

Over time, Alicia's self belief and enjoy of self grew stronger. She commenced to set bigger goals for herself, consisting of going lower back to highschool to pursue a new career. David come to be vital of her efforts and may regularly question her ability, but Alicia did not permit his remarks prevent her. She continued to claim herself and pursue her goals, even inside the face of David's negativity and shortage of emotional assist.

Eventually, Alicia determined out that she had outgrown her distorted dating with David. She had come too far to move again to the antique abusive dynamic with him. She informed him that she have become leaving him. He right now have emerge as bowled over and indignant, and engaged in blaming her at her statement. He showed no remorse, no apologies, and no duty for his conduct. But Alicia stood her ground, as she have become prepared for his response. She knew she had come to apprehend that she deserved higher in life than what David supplied her. He stood earlier than her, a person that she not recognized and not favored to be part of her life. She had resolved that she may be happier by myself than transferring ahead in lifestyles with someone like David.

Their divorce modified into acrimonious and excruciatingly painful, but Alicia had the beneficial resource of her family, her therapist, her manual organization, and her personal newfound internal energy. She had come a long way from the people-pleaser she had end up over the years of her existence. She had evolved right right right into a assured, unbiased female who knew what she desired in existence and feature emerge as a high-quality deal happier because of her decisions. She had to begin with was hoping that David need to regulate to their dating, however she diagnosed fast that he became now not capable, and he or she could not offer him with what he wanted: strength and control.

Looking lower back on her enjoy with David, and her some years of being married to him, Alicia knew that she were via lots, however she additionally knew that she had found out a outstanding deal about herself and about relationships and what they have been supposed to be: complete of love, kindness, mutual recognize, and a willingness to expand and help each other within the route of the u.S.And downs of existence. She knew that she need to in no way once more be codependent, and she vowed to commonly stand her ground for the sake of herself and her personal happiness.

Diagnosis: Narcissistic Personality Disorder (NPD)

The following is taken directly from the DSM five 5th Edition of the Diagnostic and Statistical Manual of Mental Disorders written through the American Psychiatric Association (APA) and the ebook that all licensed mental fitness practitioners use, inclusive of myself, for assessment, diagnosis, and remedy.

"A pervasive pattern of grandiosity (in fantasy or conduct), need for admiration, and lack of empathy, starting with the resource of using early maturity and discovered in a whole lot of contexts as indicated through 5 (or greater) of the following:

1. Has a grandiose experience of self-importance (e.G., exaggerates achievements and abilties, expects to be recognized as superior without commensurate achievements).

2. Is preoccupied with fantasies of countless achievement, energy, brilliance, splendor, or satisfactory love.

three. Believes that he or she is "Special" and specific and can pleasant be understood thru, or want to companion with, particular unique or highstatus humans (or establishments).

four. Requires excessive admiration.

5. Has a experience of entitlement (i.E., unreasonable expectancies of mainly favorable remedy or automatic compliance alongside with his or her expectations).

6. Is interpersonally exploitative (i.E., takes advantage of others to collect his or her very non-public ends).

7. Lacks empathy; is unwilling to recognize or discover with the emotions and desires of others.

8. Is often green with envy of others or believes that others are green with envy of her or him.

nine. Shows conceited, haughty behaviors or attitudes.

NPD includes a pervasive pattern of grandiosity, a everyday want for adoration, and a entire loss of empathy for others this is gift with the useful resource of way of the past due teens or early maturity. They frequently overvalue and overemphasize their talents and exaggerate their achievements, often imparting as bragging and pretentious.

They often will undervalue the accomplishments of others or will find out strategies to decrease or brush aside them altogether. They will outstanding associate with others who they perceive to be precise or of immoderate cost repute and feature "gifted" traits, as what they see in them is reflected in what they see in themselves. Anything plenty an awful lot less than this can no longer be tolerated. If any friends disappoint them, they immediately devalue their credentials.

How Can YouSpota Narcissist?

Here is an easy pocket guide that will help you spot commonplace tendencies for NPD:Grandiosity: Narcissists frequently have an inflated enjoy of selfimportance and agree with they may be superior to others.

Lack of empathy: Narcissists have a difficult time empathizing with others and regularly do not understand the emotions or dreams of others.

Need for admiration: Narcissists crave interest and admiration from others, often to the problem of being obsessive.

Entitlement: Narcissists agree with they'll be entitled to huge remedy and regularly take gain of others to get what they want.

Manipulation: Narcissists are skilled at manipulating others to get what they need, often the use of charm and flattery to benefit select.

Arrogance: Narcissists may be boastful and condescending, believing they're higher than others.

Lack of obligation: Narcissists often refuse to take obligation for their actions and are quick in price others.

It's important to phrase that having one or two of these inclinations could no longer typically advocate someone has a narcissistic person sickness. However, in case you study a pattern of conduct that aligns with those trends, it may be a sign that someone has a narcissistic persona. If you accept as true with you studied a person in your life has a narcissistic man or woman, it is essential to prioritize your very own properly-being and are on the lookout for for help from friends, circle of relatives, or a therapist. Choosing to stay in a dating that entails gaslighting and narcissism can create an outstanding enjoy of confusion.

When you first meet a person, test to appearance if any of the aforementioned crimson flags arise for you on your talk. Don't be dismissive and don't sweep them beneath the rug. Reach to your short pocket manual and check to make certain that the above tendencies aren't exhibited and if they'll be, irrespective of how handsome, adorable, or familiar they'll seem to you at that 2d... "Run, Forrest! Run, Forrest!" as taken from a scene from the 1994 film "Forrest Gump" starring Tom Hanks, on foot away as fast as he can from the damage that has surrounded him to get to protection.

Historical Perspectives on Nuclear Narcissism

Narcissism has been a topic of hobby for psychologists and students for hundreds of years, and they trace its roots lower returned to historical mythology. Like Narcissus within the Greek mythology legend, his story gave upward push to the concept of narcissism, which has in view that been used to explain folks who are overly preoccupied with their very own physical appearance, accomplishments, and standing.

The term "narcissism" have become first brought into current-day psychology thru the usage of Sigmund Freud inside the early twentieth century. Freud believed that narcissism have become a ordinary developmental stage that everyone bypass via within the course of youth, in which the kid is targeted on their very very own needs and dreams. However, he additionally recommended that immoderate narcissism in maturity ought to purpose pathological conduct, which include an disability to empathize with others or to shape healthy relationships.

In the mid20th century, psychologists shifted far from Freud's in advance hypothesis and ideals and started out out to define and scientifically receive narcissism as a character ailment. They diagnosed diverse person inclinations associated with NPD, together with grandiosity, a lack of empathy, and a everyday need for admiration and interest that described folks who operated interior their dating with others and the location around them.

Throughout records, narcissism has been determined in diverse bureaucracy, from the cult of individual surrounding ancient figures like Napoleon and Hitler, to modern-day figures collectively with global leaders, CEOs of critical groups, leisure stars, and common, everyday people that deal with more better styles of self-advertising and marketing and interest-searching out behaviors which may be common in modern-day society right here inside the US and sooner or later of the area.

Psychological Dynamics of Nuclear Narcissism

The mental dynamics underlying NPD offer treasured insights and are key additives to get to apprehend and find out. They embody the subsequent:

1. Grandiosity and Self-Importance: Individuals with NPD regularly have an exaggerated experience of their private achievements, competencies, and importance. They consider they'll be special and deserving of unique treatment, considering themselves superior to others.

This grandiose self-belief serves as a protection mechanism, defensive them from underlying feelings of extreme insecurity and vulnerability.

2. Fragile Self-Esteem: Paradoxically, underneath the grandiose façade, individuals with NPD frequently harbor fragile self-esteem. Their self-worth is contingent upon external validation and admiration from others. They placed out early on in their development that all validation and emotions of popularity and approval were obtained through outdoor accomplishments or particular elements outside of the "self." Any perceived criticism or rejection of that may be deeply threatening to their self-picture, primary to protecting behaviors, acting out in protest or narcissistic rage, and even in excessive office work, violence.

3. Lack of Empathy: Empathy, the functionality to understand and proportion the emotions of others, is substantially lacking in people with NPD. They war to recognize or

well known the emotions and views of others, as they'll be extensively speakme centered on their very very own needs, goals, and self-hobbies. In their developmental years, they by no means determined this important behavior for others from contributors of their own family, frequently from their dad and mom. This loss of empathy will be seen from their very non-public interactional speak with parents or parental figures, in order a younger infant, this kind set up to them.

of empathy or issue come to be now not

This confined ability for empathy can pressure private

relationships and purpose exploitative behavior.

4. Idealization and Devaluation: NPD can include a cycle of

idealizing and devaluing others. Initially, humans with NPD may also additionally idealize a person, putting them on a pedestal and admiring their developments. However, due to the fact the person fails to meet their inflated expectancies of them or challenges their fake pedestal of superiority that the narcissist has located them on, a narcissist can unexpectedly shift to devaluing and demeaning them. This cycle frequently repeats itself again and again in their relationships. They do this out of survival of self-interest for the narcissist. There isn't always any tolerance for lots a lot less than best, unique, or grand. Doing so should first-rate reduce the narcissist and the way they understand themselves.

5. Manipulation and Exploitation: Individuals with NPD might also additionally show off manipulative behaviors to hold control and dominance over others. They may additionally use attraction, flattery, or manipulation to control conditions and people to their advantage. This manipulation may be fueled thru a deep-seated want for strength and manage, serving their relentless pursuit of admiration and special treatment from others.

6. Lack of Accountability: Taking obligation for one's actions may be difficult for human beings with NPD. They might also moreover keep away from obligation and deflect blame onto others, even distorting truth to shield their self-photo. This pattern of retaining off responsibility contributes to problems in resolving conflicts and retaining healthful relationships. There is an incapability for introspection or self-reflected photo. They normally are in reality without this functionality.

By coming across the ones effective entrenched highbrow dynamics of NPD, you may start to understand the delicate, difficult complexities of this character sickness, offering depth to your expertise and losing slight on the disturbing situations and outcomes that upward thrust up from their narcissistic inclinations and behaviors.

In the following bankruptcy, we'll have a take a look at what gaslighting is, how a narcissist gaslights human beings, and why that is essential to them.

Narcissistic Abuse

This is a shape of emotional and intellectual abuse this is inflicted through a person with a narcissistic man or woman sickness. It can be specifically unfavourable and tough to understand, because the abuser manipulates and gaslights their sufferer to hold manage.

Here are a few not unusual signs and signs and signs and symptoms and signs and symptoms of narcissistic abuse internal a relationship:

Constant criticism: Narcissistic abusers often criticize their accomplice's every glide, through belittling their accomplishments or the responsibilities they're worried in, making them enjoy nugatory and meaningless. They will often reduce or refuse any guidelines or unique efforts on any depend made by means of using the victim to dissuade their enthusiasm or damper their spirit. They can criticize their patients to the thing of their sufferer losing all feelings of affection or desire for intimacy and in excessive times, purpose intense withdrawal and melancholy, even to the component of catatonia and suicidal ideation.

Blame-moving: Narcissistic abusers are specialists at deflecting blame and obligation. They may also moreover blame their partner for his or her very very own mistakes or accuse them of being too sensitive.

Gaslighting: The abuser makes the victim query their very own sanity. The abuser may also deny topics that befell or claim their associate is imagining matters.

Chapter 14: Unraveling The Concept Of Gaslighting

What Is Gaslighting?

The time period gaslighting originates from a 1938 play referred to as "Gas Light" that become later made into a movie starring Ingrid Bergman and Charles Boyer. In each the original play after which later within the movie, someone tries to steer his wife that she goes insane thru the use of manipulating the fuel lights in their domestic in addition to different items in the residence. From that time on, the word "gaslighting" has grow to be a cutting-edge term that is used inside the region of psychology and identified as a form of abuse. It takes on many office work which includes denying, twisting the reality, minimizing problems, and absolutely and surely blaming the sufferer for some thing poor that surfaces, which is often a substantial other, partner, or love hobby.

The purpose of gaslighting is to make the sufferer revel in as although they may be losing their grip on reality, or how they are decoding the location and their private contributions in the direction of "developing" chaos of their courting so you can spare the narcissist from taking any blame or obligation. The narcissist appears to have their victim be willing to fall on their personal sword, so to talk. The desires are to gain complete electricity and manage over their associate. Gaslighting can rise up in any dating, together with romantic relationships, friendships, and expert relationships. Gaslighting and narcissism are terms which is probably typically applied in psychology to provide an explanation for poisonous behaviors that cause damage to relationships, especially once they intersect with every different.

Remember that narcissism, but, refers to a persona ailment in which a person has an inflated experience of self-significance, lacks empathy, and seeks regular admiration and hobby from others. They have an exaggerated experience of entitlement, an inclination to make the most others for their very own gain, and a lack of interest for the desires and emotions of others. Though they often present as fascinating and charismatic, their conduct is self-targeted, self-absorbed, and pretty manipulative. Narcissists use gaslighting techniques to keep control over others to avoid taking responsibility for any of their moves.

GaslightingStages

The abuser will take the following moves whilst gaslighting their sufferers:

1. Create doubt: The abuser may additionally start with the useful resource of making small feedback or questioning the sufferer's memory, causing them to doubt themselves.

2. Lie: The abuser might also lie about some issue to the victim, making them doubt their personal reminiscence of sports.

3. Deny: The abuser may furthermore deny that a few factor took place or that they stated a few element, irrespective of the truth that the sufferer is privy to it to be true.

four. Twist the reality: The abuser might also twist the fact or present it in a manner that makes the victim doubt their own perception of sports.

5. Minimize the victim's feelings: The abuser can also additionally make slight of the sufferer's feelings, making them feel like their feelings are unimportant or not legitimate.

6. Turn others in opposition to the sufferer: The abuser may additionally attempt to show considered one of a type human beings within the route of the sufferer, making them experience isolated and on my own.

7. Manipulate the victim's belief of fact: The abuser might also use strategies which incorporates gaslighting, projection, or blameshifting to control the sufferer's perception of truth.

eight. Purposely create a experience of false impression: The abuser may additionally use techniques which consist of converting the problem or giving contradictory facts to create a feel of false impression inside the victim.

nine. Wear down the sufferer's vanity: The abuser can also make the sufferer sense like they're crazy or volatile, carrying down their vanity through the years.

10. Take manage: The abuser will try to take control of the victim's life for you to preserve energy and control over them.

It is important to recognize the symptoms and signs of gaslighting and are trying to find help if you are experiencing this shape of abuse. Remember that you are not on my own and that there may be help available to you. Gaslighting and exceptional forms of emotional abuse can placed on down someone's arrogance through the years in insidious procedures. The abuser also can use a number of strategies to make the victim revel in inferior or unworthy, and those processes may be hard to apprehend due to the fact they will be so often disguised as acts of love or problem.

The Terminators of Self-Esteem

Criticizing: An abuser may additionally additionally continuously criticize the sufferer's look, persona, or behavior. They may additionally make horrible remarks about the sufferer's talents, intelligence, or well absolutely worth, inflicting the sufferer to doubt themselves.

Undermining: An abuser may additionally additionally additionally undermine the sufferer's self belief by questioning their decisions, 2d-guessing their selections, or making them doubt their very personal judgment.

Isolating: An abuser may additionally isolate the victim from pals and family, making them feel like they're on my own and characteristic nowhere to show for manual.

Blaming: An abuser can also blame the victim for the whole lot that goes incorrect within the courting, even if it isn't their fault. This ought to make the sufferer sense like they may be continuously doing a little element incorrect, growing anxiety and worry within the victim.

Withholding: An abuser can also withhold affection, interest, or assist as a way of punishing the sufferer or making them feel unworthy of love and affection.

Insulting: An abuser may additionally insult the victim or name them names, making them enjoy like they are now not correct sufficient or deserving of understand.

These procedures can be specifically powerful for the abuser at the same time as they'll be used over lengthy intervals of time. The victim might also moreover start to internalize the abuser's criticisms and doubts, main to feelings of worthlessness, hopelessness, and helplessness to profound feelings of depression or maybe mind of suicide. The sufferer may additionally end up extra dependent on the abuser for validation and guide, making it greater difficult for them to break free from the relationship.

A Gaslighter's Tactics and Techniques

It's crucial to phrase that gaslighting strategies and techniques variety in depth and gaslighters may additionally use more than one techniques concurrently. These strategies cause to undermine the victim's self belief, distort their perception of truth, and preserve control over the connection. These techniques reflect realistic techniques, losing moderate at the devastating effect they may have on humans and relationships.

1. Distortion of Reality

Gaslighters often rent strategies to create confusion and make the sufferer doubt their perception of fact. They may additionally provide contradictory statistics, change their stance on an hassle, or use ambiguous language. This intentional confusion destabilizes the victim's sense of reality and reinforces the gaslighter's control. The intentional distortion or manipulation of data, occasions, or occasions to make the sufferer doubt their non-public reminiscence, perception, and sanity is deliberate and methodically carried out. The gaslighter may also moreover deny or downplay sports, trade information, or maybe fabricate statistics, major the sufferer to question their non-public version of reality.

For instance, they may say,

"You're without a doubt being paranoid."

"You are making that all up."

"You understand that isn't proper."

"You recognize that isn't what befell."

2. Gradual Erosion of Confidence

Gaslighting desires to erode the victim's self guarantee, conceitedness, and recollect of their personal judgment. By continuously invalidating the sufferer's critiques, emotions, and beliefs, the gaslighter chips away at their self-warranty. Over time, the sufferer may turn out to be increasingly reliant on the gaslighter for validation and lose their enjoy of self.

For instance, they may say,

"Do you really need to do this?"

"You recognize that couldn't be proper!"

"Are you loopy or what?" "No one might ever do that!"

3. Manipulative Techniques

Gaslighters hire a number of manipulative strategies to accumulate their goals. This can embody mendacity, deflecting blame onto the sufferer, the use of emotional manipulation to spark off guilt or disgrace, or using techniques which consist of minimizing the sufferer's emotions or exaggerating their very very own virtues. Gaslighters often excel at exploiting vulnerabilities and insecurities to advantage manipulate over their sufferers.

For instance, they'll say,

"Why did you do this?"

"You apprehend that is all due to you!"

"I could in no way try this type of thing!"

4. Isolation and Dependency

Gaslighters often isolate their sufferers from supportive relationships, together with buddies or family contributors, to boom their personal control over them. By severing those connections, the gaslighter turns into the number one, and regularly the best, deliver of validation and emotional help for the victim, making it harder for them to searching for possibility views from others or escape the manipulation. They will keep to sow seeds of doubt approximately the intentions or trustworthiness of those humans, making the victim greater reliant at the gaslighter. This isolation strengthens the gaslighter's manipulate over the sufferer's perception of truth and gets rid of the victim's opportunity to benefit one-of-a-type views from the ones they're familiar with and could typically take transport of as real with.

For example, they will say,

"You apprehend your dad and mom aren't proper for you, right?" "Now, why could you remember what your sister tells you?"

"I even have heard them speak approximately you and that they assume you aren't making real options."

"It's top notch if you best listen to me, as I understand what's notable for you."

"No one is aware of you want I do; you shouldn't accept as true with virtually anybody else."

5. Psychological Impact

Gaslighting ought to have profound intellectual results at the sufferer. Constantly wondering one's reality and experiencing self-doubt can reason anxiety, depression, and a diminished enjoy of self confidence. Victims may additionally furthermore battle with confusion, memory lapses, and a fashionable feeling of disorientation due to the gaslighter's manipulations.

For instance, they will say,

"You recognise your memory is quite awful, proper?""If I have been you, I wouldn't recollect what you spot."

"That isn't what they said or suggest; you have got that each one incorrect."

6. Power Imbalance and Control

Gaslighting establishes a energy dynamic wherein the gaslighter exerts manage over the victim's notion of fact. They come to be the authority on what is actual and what is not, wielding their effect to dominate the relationship. This strength imbalance undermines the victim's autonomy and capability to assert themselves in almost some thing they do.

"You have were given to be kidding me!"

"Where did you get that screwed up concept from?"

"Are you for actual?""No one is going to agree with you with that one!"

7. Denial and Discrediting

Gaslighters regularly deny sports or research that the victim remembers accurately. By invalidating the victim's perception of fact, the gaslighter dreams to reason them to doubt their personal reminiscence and question the accuracy in their memories.

 For instance, they may say,

"That in no way befell."

"You're making that up!"

eight. Withholding Information

Gaslighters may additionally deliberately withhold information or without issue "neglect" important info to create confusion and doubt. By controlling the drift of facts, they manipulate the victim's information of activities, making it more difficult for them to piece together the truth.

 For instance, they'll say,

"I can't accept as real with you don't recollect that!"

"That isn't what they meant!"

"Are you kidding me? That isn't always what which have come to be about in any respect!"

9. Blaming and Shifting Responsibility

Gaslighters frequently shift blame onto the sufferer, making them experience liable for the gaslighter's actions or feelings. This tactic targets to deflect duty and make the sufferer question their very non-public moves and behaviors.

 For instance, they'll say,

"If handiest you hadn't finished that, I could no longer have acted this way."

"This is all your fault. If you hadn't had accomplished that, you would not have added this on your self! That become really stupid and that is all on you!"

10. Invalidating Emotions

Gaslighters can also trivialize or disregard the sufferer's emotions, making them experience like their feelings are irrational or unwarranted. By belittling their feelings, the gaslighter undermines the sufferer's self-self belief and motives them to question the validity of their personal emotions.

For instance, they may say,

"You're too sensitive."

"You're overreacting!"

eleven. Projection

Gaslighters often task their very personal lousy developments, emotions, or behaviors onto the sufferer. For example, if the gaslighter is being untrue, they will accuse their partner of infidelity without any proof. By projecting their very personal infidelity onto the victim, the gaslighter deflects interest a long way from their private immoral dishonest conduct.

"I apprehend you're cheating on me!"

"You're sincerely mendacity to me! I can't trust you."

By exploring the interplay among narcissism and gaslighting, you could see how complicated dynamics perpetuate emotional abuse. It permits you to advantage notion into the manipulation strategies hired with the aid of using abusers and narcissists and the devastating impact gaslighting has on their patients. Furthermore, it will increase reputation about those behaviors, empowering individuals to understand and protect themselves from such toxic dynamics.

It is vital to understand the signs and symptoms and signs and symptoms and signs of emotional abuse and are searching out assist in case you are experiencing this form of abuse. Remember that you aren't on my own and that there are belongings to be had to help you regain your inner power and ruin unfastened from an abusive courting.

Trauma Bonding in Toxic Relationships

On August 23, 1973, two armed criminals, Jan-Erik Olsson and Clark Olofsson, attempted to rob a financial organization, the Kreditbanken, in Stockholm, Sweden. Their plan went awry at the same time as the police arrived, and a six-day hostage scenario followed. During this time, the hostages standard a robust connection with their captors, leading to the mental term "Stockholm Syndrome."

At the time of the robbery, the hostages exhibited behaviors that appeared counterintuitive, together with shielding and sympathizing with their captors. They advanced a revel in of loyalty and emotional attachment closer to them, even after the disturbing event had ended. This baffled every the general public and psychology professionals at that point.

The precise motives and mechanisms within the returned of Stockholm Syndrome are not noted; but, numerous theories have been proposed to present an reason for its prevalence. One idea indicates that it is a survival mechanism wherein captives or sufferers form a bond with their abusers or captors as a method to increase their probabilities of survival. By empathizing with the abuser or captors, sufferers or hostages receive as true with they may be treated extra leniently or experience reduced damage.

Another principle factors to the placement of cognitive dissonance, a intellectual phenomenon in which individuals experience soreness even as their ideals or attitudes struggle with their conduct. In the context of Stockholm Syndrome, sufferers or hostages can also additionally additionally experience cognitive dissonance even as faced with the contradictory situation of developing first-rate emotions in the route of their abusers or captors no matter the abuse or crime this is taking region. To solve this discord, they'll unconsciously regulate their perceptions and convince themselves that their abusers or captors aren't as awful as they appear like.

Stockholm Syndrome gave manner to the time period "trauma bonding," that's referred to as a deep emotional connection that develops among an abuser and a sufferer. This is frequently visible in narcissistic relationships. It usually arises when an character reports regular repetitive cycles of abuse, manipulation, and worry.

It's important to observe that Stockholm Syndrome isn't confined to the best incident in Stockholm. This can take region everywhere, at any time. It highlights the complex nature of human psychology and the capability for sudden emotional attachments and responses in immoderate situations. Living in a fairly poisonous courting along side a gaslighting, narcissistic, abusive dating can be one example.

Over time, the victim becomes emotionally depending on the abuser, and their vanity and sense of self-worth become intertwined with the abusive courting, similar to in the case test in Chapter 1 about Alicia and David.

Human relationships can be complex, and now and again people locate themselves trapped in terrible dynamics which is probably hard to peer how they sincerely are or how they're able to break out from them.

The three Characteristics ofTrauma Bonding

1. Intermittent Reinforcement: Abusive relationships frequently involve intermittent rewards and punishments, developing a powerful highbrow reinforcement cycle. This sporadic sample of powerful and awful opinions contributes to the bonding gadget.

2. Isolation and Dependency: Abusers often isolate their patients from manual networks, making it extra hard for them to are searching out for help or benefit attitude outside the abusive courting. As a give up end result, sufferers become emotionally relying on their abusers for validation and a experience of safety.

3. Survival Strategies: To deal with the trauma and abuse, victims can also increase survival

techniques at the side of dissociation, psychogenic fugue, denial, or rationalization. These strategies further beef up the bond, as sufferers rely on their abusers for their perceived survival.

EffectsofTrauma BondingonIndividuas

Cognitive Dissonance

Individuals experiencing trauma bonding frequently experience cognitive dissonance, in which they maintain contradictory ideals approximately their abusers and the abusive state of affairs. This internal struggle creates confusion, making it tough for them to understand the abusive nature of the relationship.

Chapter 15: The Interplay Between Nuclear

Narcissism and Gaslighting

S o, allow's communicate about this. These conditions do coexist with each one-of-a-type, and that they effect humans and relationships through their intersection in numerous tactics. For instance, a narcissistic partner might also deny the validity of their companion's feelings or opinions or accuse them of being overly touchy or dramatic, however conversely, insist that they may be the best one that during reality is conscious them. By doing so, the narcissistic companion can preserve manage over the connection and keep away from obligation for their personal emotionally abusive conduct.

Case Study: "Emma" and "Michael"

A center-elderly couple named Emma and Michael had been married for many years. Emma modified into a type and demanding girl who cherished Michael deeply, irrespective of his flaws. Michael, however, have become controlling and crucial of Emma. He might frequently blame her for the whole thing that went incorrect of their relationship, even supposing it wasn't her fault.

For example, if Michael forgot to pay a invoice, he might in all likelihood lash out at Emma and accuse her of now not reminding him. If Emma counseled a top notch manner of doing a little component, Michael have to dismiss her mind and inform her she modified into wrong. Over time, Emma began to doubt her non-public judgment and experience like she changed into usually doing some component incorrect.

Michael's conduct took a toll on Emma's vanity and intellectual health. She felt like she have become walking on eggshells spherical him, continually fearful of pronouncing or doing some element that could set him off. She started out out out to withdraw from friends and own family.

Despite Emma's efforts to pride Michael, now not some thing seemed to be enough. He endured to locate fault together together with her and make her experience like she modified into responsible for his or her issues. Emma began out to experience trapped within the dating, unsure of the way to break loose from the cycle of blame and criticism.

It wasn't till Emma began remedy that she located out the amount of Michael's emotional abuse. She observed approximately the concept of gaslighting and diagnosed how Michael had been manipulating her over time. With the assist of her therapist, Emma started out to set obstacles with Michael and stand up for herself. She determined out that she deserved to be dealt with with respect and kindness, and that Michael's behavior changed into now not her responsibility or her fault.

Over time, Emma's shallowness commenced to beautify, and he or she or he positioned the power to ultimately leave Michael and start a brand new lifestyles for herself. It wasn't an easy gadget however Emma determined that she changed into more potent than she imagined. She additionally located that she became no longer on my own, and that there were others who had professional comparable forms of abuse. With time and assist, Emma became capable of heal from the accidents of her beyond and create a brighter future for herself. Her preference have become to live a happier life by myself than to be forced into staying with someone who may also simplest hold to abuse her.

In addition to the use of gaslighting strategies to govern their sufferers, narcissists may also be more likely to engage in gaslighting conduct for themselves. Narcissists have an inflated enjoy of self-importance and a belief that their perspective is the exceptional valid one. They disregard or ignore the perspectives of others, which includes their partners, and call for that their version of sports is the best authentic one. This can bring about confusion and doubt inside the minds in their companions, as they begin to question their non-public perceptions and research.

The interaction among narcissism and gaslighting is notable and is more often intertwined.

Sharing the Common Thread

With an selfish popularity, each narcissism and gaslighting percent a common thread inside the dating of manipulation and manipulate. Narcissists have an inherent want for electricity and control over others, and gaslighting offers them with a manner to claim dominance. They use gaslighting techniques to manipulate their victims' notion of truth, making sure that their model of occasions prevails and that they keep manage over their victims.

Narcissists non-public an overinflated experience of self-importance and keep in mind they are superior to others. This grandiosity fuels their gaslighting behaviors, as they experience entitled to control and manage the narrative to align with their self-perception. Gaslighting allows them to hold their delusions of superiority even as undermining the victim's selfesteem.

Both narcissism and gaslighting contain a loss of empathy. Narcissists war to apprehend and validate the feelings and experiences of others, focusing normally on their very very own dreams and goals. Gaslighting reinforces this loss of empathy, because the narcissist dismisses or invalidates the victim's feelings and stories, prioritizing their personal time table.

Commonly sporting out idealization and devaluation cycles in relationships, they will to begin with idealize their patients, showering them with affection and admiration. However, because of the truth the sufferer fails to fulfill their unrealistic expectations or demanding conditions their superiority, the narcissist may additionally shift to devaluation, using gaslighting strategies to undermine the sufferer's self-worth and preserve manage.

Narcissists have fragile arrogance beneath their grandiose façades. They rely carefully on out of doors validation to strengthen their self confidence, and any perceived grievance or danger to their superiority may be deeply unsettling. Gaslighting turns into a tool for self-maintenance, permitting narcissists to defend their fragile conceitedness via distorting reality and moving blame onto others. It allows them to hold their selfperception as advanced and infallible.

Gaslighting allows the strength imbalance in relationships with narcissists. The victim becomes increasingly more relying on the narcissist for validation and a revel in of reality, while the narcissist keeps control over the narrative. This dependency strengthens the narcissist's feature and makes it extra tough for the sufferer to interrupt free from the manipulation.

The intermittent lower decrease returned-and-forth reinforcement of first rate and horrible behaviors from the abuser or narcissist, coupled with the victim's confusion and self-doubt, can create a robust emotional attachment. This bond can make it difficult for the sufferer to completely detach from the connection, despite the reality that they will be aware of the abusive or crook dynamics. It is rather tough to have an outdoor mindset at the same time as your abuser is the person that is meant to love and deal with you, like a decide or a partner.

Other factors that they percentage embody the subsequent:

Reinforcement of Narcissistic Supply

Narcissistic supply refers to the eye, admiration, and validation that narcissists crave. Gaslighting permits narcissists to control others into imparting this supply name for that they are continuously pushed to acquire. By undermining the sufferer's conceitedness, instilling self-doubt, and controlling the narrative, narcissists can maintain a constant circulate constantly looking to top off, similar to trying to top off their internal gasoline tank.

elicit the famous reactions and

of narcissistic supply they will be

Intertwined Patterns

Narcissism and gaslighting regularly appear in intertwined styles indoors relationships. Narcissists use gaslighting to devalue and manipulate their sufferers and through invalidating their reviews, feelings, and views, narcissists undermine the sufferer's self perception and installation a energy dynamic that enhances their narcissistic inclinations.

Impact on the Victim's Perception

Gaslighting via a narcissist can deeply impact the victim's notion of reality. The repeated manipulation and distortion of reality can lead the victim to impeach their private judgment, reminiscence, and sanity. The gaslighting procedures hired by using narcissists can erode the victim's conceitedness, create confusion, and foster a dependence on the narcissist for validation and steering.

Complex Emotional Abuse

The nexus of narcissism and gaslighting creates a complicated shape of emotional abuse. The aggregate of the narcissist's selfcentered behavior, manipulation tactics, and gaslighting techniques can result in profound emotional misery, anxiety, and self-doubt for the victim.

What Is the Impact of Gaslighting and Narcissism Together?

The effect of gaslighting and narcissism collectively on humans and relationships is massive and may be catastrophic. Gaslighting reasons patients to experience confused, demanding, and isolated. They begin to doubt their private perceptions and reminiscences and may even sense as even though they may be going crazy. This can cause a lack of conceitedness and self-self belief, in addition to a sense of powerlessness and helplessness. Victims of gaslighting may additionally moreover experience as even though they cannot bear in mind their very non-public thoughts and emotions and may end up increasingly relying on their abuser for validation and approval.

Impacton Individuals andSocieties

OnIndividuals

Emotional Distress

Narcissism and gaslighting can motive incredible emotional misery for folks that are subjected to them. Victims can also revel in anxiety, depression, low arrogance, and feelings of worthlessness because of the manipulative strategies and normal invalidation in their critiques and feelings.

Self-Doubt and Identity Erosion

Narcissism and gaslighting can erode an person's experience of self and self-worth. Victims may moreover question their very very own ideals, values, and abilities due to the reality the gaslighter systematically undermines their self belief and distorts their truth. This can result in a loss of identity and a diminished enjoy of private business organization.

Relationship Difficulties

Individuals who've been uncovered to narcissism and gaslighting often face challenges in forming and preserving healthful relationships. Manipulation and emotional abuse can depart lasting scars, making it hard to consider others, explicit emotions openly, and set up boundaries.

Isolation and Social Withdrawal

Victims of gaslighting and narcissistic abuse also can feel isolated and withdraw from social interactions. The gaslighter frequently seeks to isolate their victims, making them extra relying on them for validation and assist. This isolation can result in a experience of loneliness and make it extra hard for the character to seeking out assist or resource.

Impaired Decision-Making

Gaslighting and narcissism can impair an individual's ability to make selections with a bit of success. Victims may additionally moreover moreover doubt their very very very own judgment and rely on the gaslighter's critiques and steering, principal to a lack of autonomy and personal corporation. This have to have long-time period effects for their private and professional lives.

OnSociety

Interpersonal Conflict

Narcissism and gaslighting interior society can make contributions to extended interpersonal battle. When human beings prioritize their private goals and control others to keep manipulate, it creates a breeding ground for anxiety, distrust, and discord amongst people and social businesses.

Erosion of Trust

Narcissism and gaslighting can erode take into account inner societies. When human beings engage in manipulative behaviors and deform reality to wholesome their very non-public schedule, it turns into difficult to rely on others and set up a foundation of agree with. This can weaken social bonds and avoid collaboration and cooperation.

Disruption of Social Systems

In extreme times, the prevalence of narcissism and gaslighting internal a society can disrupt guidelines, social shape, political electricity, structures, and establishments. Manipulative individuals also can upward push to positions of first-rate electricity and control of organizations, states, and worldwide places and abuse their authority, essential to the erosion of democratic techniques, justice structures, and social cohesion.

Normalization of Toxic Behaviors

If narcissism and gaslighting come to be normalized inside a society, it may perpetuate a subculture of emotional abuse and manipulation. This normalization can preclude private growth, empathy, and the improvement of healthy relationships, fundamental to prolonged-lasting societal outcomes for everyone.

Inequality and Exploitation

Narcissistic people can also moreover make the maximum and control others for non-public gain, contributing to extended societal inequality. The recognition on selfimportance and dismiss for others' nicely-being can lead to the exploitation of inclined humans or marginalized agencies, perpetuating social injustices.

Understanding the outcomes of narcissism on people and societies is essential for elevating interest and selling wholesome relationships and social structures. By addressing the ones influences, you could shed mild on the significance of recognizing and addressing those poisonous behaviors to foster non-public increase, resilience, and a extra compassionate society to boom to all of humanity.

Chapter 16: Codependency: Enabling And
Sustaining the Cycle

Case Study: "Lena"

Lena had continuously been the great to attend to others. As a toddler, she end up constantly the peacemaker in her own family, making sure her siblings have been given alongside and that her dad and mom had been happy. She carried this function into her maturity, in which she have emerge as the primary caregiver for her ageing parents and her youngsters.

Lena prided herself on being reliable, reliable, and selfless. She felt a revel in of purpose and validation from being desired through others. But over time, Lena started to revel in overwhelmed, and he or she have turn out to be inexperienced with envy. She changed into constantly setting others' dreams earlier than her personal, and she felt like nobody modified into either worried about her nicely-being or ever supplied to help her.

Lena's husband Jake become regularly absent and he grow to be emotionally a ways off. He labored prolonged hours and did now not appear to recognize or admire Lena's efforts for all that she did. Lena felt unappreciated and unsupported, but she did now not apprehend a way to invite for what she desired. She did not need to appear selfish or needy and she or he felt it became her characteristic to assist others.

A friend of hers had encouraged a e book on codependency and at the beginning, Lena modified into reluctant; she didn't see herself as someone with addiction or dependency problems, but the extra she had been given into the ebook, she started to emerge as aware about a number of the tendencies in herself which started out to alarm her.

The e-book went on to give an cause for that codependency modified into now not approximately being addicted to a substance, however greater about being addicted to searching after others. Codependent people have a propensity to neglect approximately their personal goals in pick out of others and regularly conflict with boundaries, communication, and self-care.

Lena soon started out to revel in that the e-book changed into describing her lifestyles. She found out that her enjoy of identification and self esteem had come to be actually tied to her position as a caregiver. She felt like she couldn't be happy except others have been happy spherical her, and that she through the use of a few technique felt that she changed into answerable for everybody else's emotions and revel in of well-being.

As Lena endured her have a have a take a look at, she started out out to revel in a feel of remedy. She positioned out that she wasn't on my own in her struggles and that there has been a name for what she emerge as experiencing. She additionally determined out that codependency have become some issue that could be dealt with and conquer.

The e-book furnished Lena with equipment and techniques for putting limitations, talking assertively, and prioritizing her personal desires. Lena commenced to exercise these capabilities in her relationships with others. She observed to mention no even as she needed to, and to invite for help whilst she wanted it.

Lena's new behavior with own family and pals as it emerged modified into met with resistance. Her husband did not understand why she regarded bored with looking after him. Her dad and mom have grow to be frustrated that she wasn't capable of commit as a super deal time and electricity to them as she used to.

But she endured. She started out to slowly prioritize her very very personal dreams and he or she discovered out the manner to encompass and exercise self-care. She sought assist and help to paintings thru her codependency issues and Lena began to construct a stronger sense of self esteem.

Over time, Lena's relationships started out to enhance. Some of her friends moved on, as it seemed they simply didn't apprehend the modifications that had taken place and refused to in truth be given the new Lena. But her husband Jake regularly began to recognize and understand her and slowly they commenced out to paintings on and repair what became desired for each different's goals. Lena's parents commenced to slowly come spherical to respect her new suggested obstacles and feature come to be more self-enough and much much less needy of her. Lena's kids also benefited from their mother's newfound self belief and self-assuredness as they started out to workout the same subjects that Lena turn out to be getting to know with their non-public circles of buddies.

Lena located out that by using way of understanding the importance of looking after herself that she modified into capable to take care of others greater effectively while it have come to be suitable. She not felt like she needed to sacrifice her non-public wishes and properly-being to help others or get their love or nod of approval. She may be there for others when it have become needed, however even though be able to be there for herself without sacrificing her private desires.

Understanding codependency had opened Lena's eyes to a ultra-modern manner of living and thriving. She located out that she no longer had to be a martyr or a constant peacemaker inside the family or together collectively with her buddies to be glad. She is probably her personal person, collectively together with her very very personal goals and desires. She must stay a fulfilling and gratifying existence, at the same time as furthermore being there for the people she loved. It have turn out to be a tough technique at the begin for Lena; it changed into distant places to her to set up a latest pattern of communication, but with staying power and diligence and living with the feeling of discomfort earlier than her new self emerged, it turn out to be all so properly

properly worth it. Her existence modified into a lot happier as a give up give up end result.

The Enabling Component

This refers back to the conduct of supporting or accommodating the terrible patterns of some other individual, often to the detriment of one's private well-being. In the context of codependency, allowing is a key issue that sustains the cycle of dysfunctional relationships.

Here are some factors to do not forget:

Emotional Caretaking: Codependent people frequently take on the placement of emotional caretaker of their relationships. They experience chargeable for the properly-being and happiness of others, particularly the character displaying narcissistic conduct. They also can constantly located their very personal dreams aside to meet the dreams of the possibility person, allowing their conduct thru taking on excessive responsibility.

Rescuing and Fixing: Codependents can also have a sturdy desire to rescue or healing the troubles of the narcissistic man or woman. They take delivery of as real with that thru continuously providing resource and answers, they could change or decorate the individual. This conduct lets in the narcissist's reliance on the codependent and reinforces the cycle of disorder.

Enabling Manipulation: Codependents regularly permit the manipulative techniques of the narcissist. They can also moreover make excuses for their conduct, cowl up their errors, or receive blame on their behalf. By doing so, they defend the narcissist from facing consequences, permitting the manipulative patterns to persist.

Sacrificing Personal Boundaries: Codependents often sacrifice their very own boundaries to cope with the dreams and wishes of the narcissistic man or woman. They can also tolerate disrespectful or abusive behavior, overlook about their very very very own nicely-being, and suppress their private emotions to maintain the connection. This loss of obstacles lets in the narcissist to keep their self-focused conduct.

Validation and Reinforcement: Codependents play a crucial function in validating and reinforcing narcissistic conduct. They also can provide constant hobby, admiration, and approval, seeking out to pride the narcissist and avoid battle. This validation serves as a praise for the narcissist's behavior, reinforcing their experience of entitlement and control over the codependent character.

Chapter 17: Understanding Codependency And

Its Link to Narcissism: How Do

They Intersect?

Codependency and narcissism describe patterns of behavior that bring about poisonous and dangerous relationships. Codependency refers to a pattern of behavior in which someone will become excessively reliant on others for validation, self-worth, and emotional help.

Take the following codependency test to look if any of this resonates with you:

Codependency Test

Instructions:

Answer the subsequent questions with a "sure" or "no" response based to your feelings, thoughts, and behaviors. Be honest with yourself and avoid overthinking your responses.

1. Do you often positioned different human beings's want and goals before your very very personal?

2. Do you conflict to specific your non-public need and desires? Three. Do you enjoy responsible or egocentric even as you're saying no to someone?

4. Do you revel in answerable for first-rate human beings's feelings or nicely- being?

5. Do you war with making selections for your self?

6. Do you find out your self in relationships with people who have addictive or controlling behaviors?

7. Do you've got a difficult time placing boundaries with others? Eight. Do you sense worrying or uncomfortable whilst a person else is disillusioned or irritated with you?

nine. Do you frequently forget about your non-public feelings on the way to maintain the peace with others?

10. Do you have got problem announcing "I love you" or showing affection to others?

Scoring:

Count the quantity of "certain" responses to decide your codependency rating. If you responded positive to five or greater questions, you could have codependent tendencies. If you spoke back sure to eight or extra questions, it's miles probably that you battle with codependency.

It is critical to bear in mind that this check isn't always a formal analysis and need to no longer be used to replace expert medical recommendation or remedy. If you are struggling with codependency or any highbrow fitness issues, please are searching out the steerage of a licensed mental fitness professional.

The Roots of Narcissism and Codependency

Let's have a have a have a look at how codependency can effects motive matching up with a narcissist, and the effect this dynamic should have on individuals and relationships.

Codependency is regularly rooted in early adolescents stories, in conjunction with a loss of emotional help, nurturing, or validation from their mother and father or caregivers. Codependent human beings can also struggle with faded levels of vanity, emotions of inadequacy, and a want for outdoor validation. They research from an early age that they get their immoderate pleasant reinforcement and a faux enjoy of affection and protection by means of manner of serving or helping others, typically individuals in their circle of relatives. They deliver to people who take.

This behavioral sample becomes entrenched as to their perceived cost that they provide to others. They frequently have trouble putting barriers, announcing no, and prioritizing any of their very personal dreams and desires. Developing into adulthood, codependency can motive a pattern of behavior wherein a person becomes excessively targeted at the wishes and dreams of others, frequently to the detriment in their very very own nicely-being.

Narcissism, conversely, is frequently rooted in a lack of emotional assist and validation in younger people as properly. However, narcissists address this lack of manual in a very particular way than codependents. Rather than turning into overly focused at the desires of others, narcissists become overly centered on their personal needs and desires. They also can make the most and manage the codependent to get what they need. They use gaslighting approaches to manipulate and manipulate the codependent, denying the validity of their emotions and reports and insisting that their non-public attitude is the best valid one. Narcissists interact in emotional or mental abuse, together with belittling, criticizing, or humiliating their partner. Over time, this erodes the codependent's experience of self.

While codependency and narcissism can also additionally appear to be opposites, they without a doubt result in complementing each unique in a courting, as toxic as this is. Codependent humans can be interested in narcissists due to the fact they may be interested by the self guarantee, air of thriller, and attention-attempting to find behavior of narcissists but tragically, to their personal detriment. Narcissists, however, can be attracted and interested in codependents because of the reality the codependents are much more likely to offer the consistent interest, admiration, and validation that narcissists crave. This is wherein they're capable of top off their inner gasoline tank any time they want.

The codependent and narcissistic dynamic may be dangerous and toxic for both parties concerned. Codependents can also furthermore end up enmeshed with the narcissist, dropping sight of their personal dreams and goals within the way. They can also moreover come to be overly focused on meeting the wishes and needs of the narcissist, often predominant to their very own lack of self. This can purpose a lack of conceitedness, self-self notion, and a feel of personal identity.

Finally Breaking Free—Take the Steps to Break the Cycle

Breaking unfastened from the codependent and narcissistic duo dynamic dance can be difficult, but it's miles viable.

It consists of 4 steps that every birthday celebration wants to make:

1. Recognize that the connection isn't healthful and that adjustments want to be made.

2. Requires that each sports need to be inclined to renowned their feature in the dynamic and to paintings on converting their behaviors.

3. It's vital for the codependent to art work on placing obstacles, pronouncing no, and

prioritizing their non-public desires and desires.

4. Narcissists need to artwork on growing empathy, treating others with respect and compassion, and reading to take obligation for his or her moves.

This final step can be found out, but enforcing it into actual-life packages is difficult, and it is essential to understand entering into that this very last step frequently consequences in failure. I commonly try to constantly keep the motto: "Hope for the exquisite, but put together and plan for the worst." Don't delude or lessen this very last step. And remedy also can be an effective tool for addressing codependency and narcissism together. One can benefit from remedy to assist increase a more potent sense of self, set barriers, and artwork on building greater wholesome relationships. Either agency or 1:1 remedy is right, and now not the use of a greater than 6–8 participants in a fixed led by means of a certified licensed highbrow clinical physician.

To recap, codependency is a intellectual situation that often develops in relationships wherein one individual well-knownshows narcissistic inclinations and the other person is characterized by way of using an excessive reliance on others for his or her self esteem, their powerful want for approval, and an disability to installation healthy barriers.

Here are some extra bullet factors to endure in mind:

Definition of Codependency

Codependency refers to a pattern of conduct wherein an man or woman excessively relies on every other man or woman for emotional, physical, or psychological dreams. Codependent humans frequently prioritize the desires and desires of others over their non-public, sacrificing their personal nicely-being inside the process. This sample of conduct is rooted in low vanity, a worry of abandonment, and a distorted experience of self-worth.

Enabling Narcissistic Behavior

Codependency and narcissism frequently move hand in hand. The codependent individual will become an enabler for the narcissist, quality their wishes, appeasing their demands, and continuously attempting to find their approval. This aggregate dynamic feeds into the narcissist's desire for control and validation, perpetuating their self-focused behavior however compliments the choice of the codependent to be a people-pleaser and serve the goals of another.

Lack of Boundaries

Codependents conflict to set up and located into impact wholesome obstacles in their private, regularly due to a fear of rejection, abandonment, or loss of affection. This lack of barriers hurries up and permits the narcissist's manipulative strategies, as they start to make the most the codependent person's willingness to sacrifice their very own desires. The codependent individual can also moreover tolerate emotional abuse, manipulation, and overlook in the pursuit of preserving the connection.

Self-Worth Tied to Validation

Codependents typically derive their self confidence from the validation they gather from others, in particular the narcissistic character. They are searching out for regular reassurance and approval, relying on the narcissist's remarks to validate their own rate. This reliance on outside validation reinforces the energy dynamics in the courting and perpetuates the codependent patterns.

Fear of Autonomy

Codependency is frequently rooted in a fear of autonomy and the belief that one can't feature independently. The codependent individual also can have an immoderate want for the narcissist's steerage and path, feeling disturbing or out of region when no longer under their partner's manage. This worry of autonomy becomes a using pressure in retaining the relationship, regardless of the reality that it's far unfavorable to their non-public nicely-being.

Reinforcement of Narcissistic Supply

Codependents inadvertently provide the narcissist with a regular bypass of narcissistic supply. Their willingness to sacrifice their non-public wishes and validate the narcissist's ego feeds into the narcissist's self-centered behavior. The codependent individual's relentless assist and permitting similarly perpetuate the narcissist's sense of entitlement and manipulate.

Healing and Breaking the Cycle

Recognizing the hyperlink among codependency and narcissism is essential for humans to interrupt loose from poisonous relationships and heal. Developing self-esteem, placing and imposing limitations, and searching for help are essential steps in breaking the codependent patterns. It is crucial for codependent humans to prioritize their personal properly-being and shift their awareness from outdoor validation to self-care.

By exploring the hyperlink amongst codependency and narcissism, you may see the complicated dynamics that perpetuate the ones toxic relationships. It offers a deeper records of the interplay amongst those two situations and empowers people to apprehend and cope with codependent behaviors.

Breaking the cycle of codependency in a narcissistic dating can be difficult but empowering, and may be completed through the years with perseverance and staying power.

Here are a few one-of-a-kind critical issues for overcoming it:

1. First, Recognize the Patterns: The first step is to recognize the codependent patterns and

acknowledge the impact they've in your well-being. Become aware about the permitting behaviors, sacrificing of boundaries, and the emotional dependency that perpetuates the relational cycle. Understanding the dynamics at play is vital for beginning alternate.

What is the sample in your dating? (Enabling? Sacrificing? Emotional dependency?)

2. Seek Support: Reach out for help from depended on buddies,

family, or a certified therapist who can offer easy guidance and validation. Share your critiques and concerns with individuals who can provide a smooth angle and aid your adventure toward breaking free from the codependent cycle. Who is your help?

3. Build Self-Esteem: Focus on rebuilding your shallowness and self confidence independent of the narcissistic person you are worried with. Engage in sports activities that supply you delight, find out your passions, and

cultivate a revel in of autonomy and selfidentity. Seek validation from inner and workout selfcompassion to counteract the outdoor validation you may have relied on in the past.

How will you validate your self? What is your passion? What is your revel in of identification?

Chapter 18: Boundaries

Boundaries are absolutely about you and not a person else in the hopes that you could alternate their conduct. Boundaries are all approximately letting others recognize what you are comfortable with and what you aren't. They help you allow others recognize from the very outset who you are and what makes up your morals, values, and basically everything this is about you.

How to Set Boundaries

When coping with a narcissist, setting new limitations can be surprisingly hard as they may be resistive at every preliminary attempt you're making. This may be a bizarre new courting for them. And this is one fashion that they'll be surely unexpected with and could probable be very unhappy with the very last results as they will soon come to discover that the energy and manage they as quickly as possessed over their associate has come to a eternal prevent.

Relationships and th e roles they play are like a infant's cell this is frequently located placing from the ceiling over a crib. When one piece of the cell shifts, all special quantities shift as nicely until they stabilize yet again. When a breeze comes into the room and shifts the placing fragile mobile over again, the elements of the mobile will shift all once more. It is critical to apprehend that as one shifts their limitations, similar to the infant's mobile, all certainly one of a type quantities of the relationship will shift once more, a few for the great and others for undesired consequences. Again, time and endurance.

The following are steps you could take to assist set your new obstacles:

1. Establish Your Boundaries

Set and put into effect wholesome barriers inside the courting. Clearly talk your wishes, expectations, and barriers to the narcissistic person. Be prepared for resistance, as they will face up to or push towards the limits you've set. Stay enterprise in prioritizing your properly-being and give a boost to your limitations continuously with consequences.

What are your obstacles going to be and with whom?

Again, here is a place wherein many are uncomfortable retaining their barriers and speakme with others. It is critical which you be vigilant of a while, location, and ranges of willpower. Being assertive isn't much like being aggressive. Just the statistics—in case you placed them available, they grow to be independent. If someone else takes offense, then allow that be their problem and now not yours. Give yourself time to workout. It turns into more snug for you the greater you exercising.

Here are a few techniques to say no to a person and mean it without coming off as offensive or rude:

Plain and simple: "No."

"You recognize, that clearly doesn't paintings for me but thanks except."

"I am no longer willing to try this, however I am willing to do that…""I'm no longer going to try this, however I am willing to do that…""You recognize, that actually doesn't experience proper for me."

"You comprehend, I'm no longer good enough with that.""Perhaps all all over again."

"I want to mention no to that, however thanks except for asking me.""No, thank you."

"No, I could alternatively not; that definitely isn't who I am." 2. Define Your Boundaries

Before you can set limitations, you want to be clean on what your limitations are. Think about what conduct is unacceptable to you and what you are willing to tolerate. Write down your limitations and be particular.

three. Communicate Your Boundaries

Once you've got defined your limitations, it's time to speak them to the narcissist. Be easy and company at the same time as speaking your limitations and avoid getting emotional or conducting arguments. If you discover yourself beginning to engage in a problem, prevent and take a spoil and are to be had lower lower back to it later. Repeat the equal manner if it takes place again. The vital component is to be organisation whilst speaking the limits that you want to installation.

four. Stick to Your Boundaries

Narcissists are appeared for trying out barriers, so it is critical to paste to your barriers as quick as you've got got communicated them. If the narcissist attempts to push your barriers or bulldoze them over, remind them of your expectancies and the consequences inside the occasion that they preserve to transport your obstacles. But you want to be prepared to conform with thru with any consequences to their alternatives or behaviors, in any other case they may keep no price. In existence, everyone need to be responsible to the picks and consequences we make in our lives.

What are your expectations from them?

What are the outcomes for them which you are inclined to preserve thru if they go your boundaries? Be practical and be organized to examine through.

How do you believe you studied they'll initially reply to them? Be prepared...

five. Stay Consistent With Your Boundaries

Consistency is high while putting limitations with a narcissist. If you waiver or provide in to their needs, they'll see it as a signal of weakness and may hold to push your boundaries, and they'll see your conduct as intermittently reinforcing opportunities for their conduct which normally outcomes in overpowering, manipulate, and manipulation.

Do you be aware any resistance from them and what's it?

Four Basic Rules forEstablishingBoundaries

Remember to use your "I" statements (I experience, I locate, I will, I want, I desire, I would really like, and lots of others.), and in doing so, this truly directs others what you are willing to do and what you are not inclined to do.

There are 4 basic suggestions for the way to set up barriers with others: 1. Clearly nation regardless of the hassle is. Do no longer be vague or ambiguous.

For example:

"When you are saying unkind matters to me at my fee, it's far cruel." 2. Be very particular. Do not be fashionable or vague on your conveyance.

For instance:

"You threw that tumbler proper in front of me, which fearful me, and then you definitely definately yelled at me that it wasn't a large deal and also you said I emerge as overreacting."

3. Use your "I…" statements. Using your I statements conveys how it's far affecting you physically, mentally, emotionally, in addition to in exceptional tactics.

For instance:

"When you continued to make jokes at me in public when I asked you to prevent, I felt humiliated. If you're making jokes at me in public again, I will upward thrust up and leave."

four. Set business enterprise, believable effects. Choose ones which may be lasting and that you could look at through on.

For example: Instead of announcing, "If you spend cash that we don't have all another time, I will in no manner speak to you."

Say, "If you gamble away our tough -earned cash over again after we have had many discussions about the seriousness of this and the manner it impacts our ability to thrive, and after you've got were given agreed that you won't gamble, I will depart."

It's important to look at that placing obstacles with a narcissist might not result in on the spot exchange. Narcissists are often proof against exchange and can attempt to hold their conduct regardless of your efforts to set limitations. However, sticking on your obstacles similarly to the results for breaking them will let you regain your revel in of manage and self-worth, and might eventually motive changes within the narcissist's behavior.

Chapter 19: Here Are A Few Not Unusual

Psychological Resilience and

Healing

Questions About Dealing With a Narcissist

Here are a few common questions that those handling a narcissist of their lives regularly have.

Can YouChange a Narcissist?

The easy technique to this is "no." Dealing with a narcissist is tough and may be truely draining. It can take a toll on your intellectual health and your complete nicely-being. It is important to renowned that even though you cannot change the narcissist, you could exchange the manner you respond to them. Developing inner power, resilience, and restoration will permit you to navigate the annoying situations of both being in a dating with a narcissist, or ultimately breaking loose from the dynamic if you so choose.

Is It Possible for a Narcissistto Have aSuccessful RelationshipWithTheir Partner?

Though it is unusual, they will, however it often requires huge art work at the a part of each occasions. Narcissists' achievement of improvement and exchange will often be determined based totally on their degree of impairment (Diagnostic and Statistical Manual of Mental Disorders Table 2 Level of Personality Functioning Scale DSM 5 fifth Edition APA) and can be assessed as 0, which means that little or no impairment; 1, some impairment; 2, mild impairment; 3, extreme impairment; to four, excessive impairment. The closing categories have horrible consequences of preserving a fulfillment relationships or forming healthy, enjoyable relationships because of their tendency to prioritize their very private needs and goals in the main else and those of others.

In order for a narcissist to have a a success courting, they need to be inclined to widely known and address their complex conduct.

This regularly calls for remedy or superb sorts of professional help to help the narcissist understand the effect of their behavior on their companion and to growth greater wholesome coping mechanisms.

At the same time, the partner of a narcissist want to moreover be willing to set obstacles and rise up for themselves. They should be willing to mention their very very own dreams and desires, even supposing it manner pushing yet again in competition to the narcissist's attempts to govern or manipulate them.

Ultimately, whether or not or not a narcissist could have a a hit courting with their accomplice is predicated upon at the willingness of both activities to paintings collectively to create a wholesome and balanced dynamic. It is not not viable, however it calls for masses of try and dedication to increase and trade.

Can a NarcissistCommitto a Relationship?

Narcissists can determine to a courting, however their commitment won't be the same as a person who isn't always a narcissist. Narcissists have a tendency to be extra targeted on their private needs and desires and might view relationships as a way to an stop—a manner to gain hobby, admiration, or different styles of validation.

In a few instances, a narcissist can be dedicated to a relationship because it serves their very very own dreams—as an instance, inside the occasion that they have got a accomplice who gives financial or emotional assist. However, their strength of mind may not be based completely totally on a true choice to build a wholesome and at the same time fun courting.

Narcissists additionally have a propensity to have a difficult time with intimacy and vulnerability, that would make it difficult for them to certainly decide to a courting. They may be much more likely to interact in behaviors that undermine the connection, which include dishonest or being deceitful, including gaslighting techniques, and may war to take obligation for their movements or make large adjustments.

Overall, at the same time as a narcissist can be capable of committing to a relationship, it's miles critical to method such relationships with warning and to be aware about the capability disturbing conditions and purple flags related to narcissistic behavior.

Do AllNarcissists Engage inCriminalorUnethcal Behavior?

While it is not continually real that each one narcissists will end up in jail or have interaction in unlawful behaviors, a few research have recommended that people with narcissistic individual tendencies may be more likely to interact in crook hobby or unethical behavior.

Narcissists have a tendency to prioritize their personal desires and wishes above others, number one to a disregard for social norms and regulations. Additionally, they will lack empathy and guilt, making it easier for them to justify their moves even though they damage others.

One take a look at determined that people with immoderate stages of narcissism had been more likely to engage in severa sorts of unethical conduct, inclusive of cheating, mendacity, and stealing. Another test positioned that humans with excessive degrees of narcissism were much more likely to engage in illegal sports activities which include drug use and theft.

However, it's miles critical to note that now not every body with narcissistic inclinations may have interaction in illegal or unethical behavior. Many might also in reality have problems of their relationships and interactions with others, but though manipulate to steer useful lives. It in the end relies upon on a whole lot of character factors and situations in addition to the extent of diploma of effect.

ShouldIStay orLeave?

Regarding whether or not to head away the relationship or live in it, regardless of how long you've got got been within the relationship, there can be no one-length-fits-all solution, and it is also as much as the character to make this desire. Additionally, it is predicated upon at the specific situations and the extent of toxicity and severity of the narcissist and their conduct inside the dating. Leaving may be the tremendous choice if the narcissistic behavior is immoderate, abusive, and negatively impacting your properly-being or violating your protection or the ones of your kids. Leaving the connection is complicated and comes with its very personal stressful situations, especially if there are youngsters concerned or economic difficulties, regulations, or dependencies.

Ultimately, the selection to go away or live ought to prioritize your safety and well-being first. If you pick out to live, it's far important to keep working on your self, hold to set enterprise limitations, and are searching for assist to hold your personal emotional, religious, and mental fitness.

Remember, breaking the cycle of codependency is a adventure that calls for staying strength, self-compassion, and perseverance. It will most simply incorporate u.S.A.And downs, however with effort and time, you can regain your revel in of self.

Tips for Dealing With a Narcissist

If making a decision to live together in conjunction with your narcissistic companion, right here are some recommendations for developing strengths interior your self to acquire resilience and restoration:

Build a manual community: Surround your self with individuals who are supportive, loving, and annoying. Reach out to pals, family individuals, or a therapist for useful resource and guidance. Having a guide network can provide you with a feel of validation and will assist you to enjoy much less remoted and on my own.

Develop independence: Work on growing your independence and autonomy. Focus on building a guide community out of doors of narcissistic relationships. Cultivate friendships, pursue character interests, and spend money on non-public increase. Increasing your independence lessens the emotional reliance at the narcissistic individual and empowers you to make options that prioritize your properly-being and what's important to you.

Practice self-care: Take care of your self emotionally, and mentally. This might also moreover furthermore contain physical,

project sports sports which you revel in, along side interests or workout, getting enough sleep, ingesting a wholesome weight loss plan, and schooling mindfulness or meditation. Self-care will assist you to to revel in extra targeted, grounded, and resilient.

Set boundaries: It is important to set barriers with a narcissist to defend your very very own well-being. This can also moreover moreover comprise saying no to requests or wishes that feel unreasonable or intrusive, placing limits on how thousands time you spend with the narcissist, or refusing to have interaction in arguments or confrontations. Setting obstacles assist you to to revel in greater empowered and in control of the situation.

Learn to apprehend gaslighting: Gaslighting is a tactic that narcissists use to manipulate and control others. It includes denying the validity of each special man or woman's evaluations or emotions and insisting that their very very personal mind-set is the most effective valid one. Learning to apprehend gaslighting will assist you to feel more assured for your very non-public memories and to upward push up for yourself whilst critical.

Build your self-esteem: Narcissists often try to tear down the conceitedness of others a very good manner to preserve manage. Building your very very very own conceitedness will can help you to feel more assured, empowered, and much much less prone to the narcissist's methods. This may additionally include walking with a therapist, training selfcompassion, and attractive in sports activities activities that make you sense appropriate about yourself.

Practice assertiveness: Being assertive manner repute up for your self and expressing your want and goals in a smooth and direct way. Learning to be assertive allow you to to experience greater on pinnacle of things of the state of affairs and to set boundaries that guard your non-public properly-being. This may additionally additionally additionally contain training assertiveness competencies with a therapist or in a useful resource organisation.

Seek professional help: It can be useful to looking for expert help, collectively with remedy or counseling, to allow you to your adventure of restoration. A therapist can offer you with manual, steerage, machine, and tried-and-actual techniques tailored on your precise state of affairs for coping with the annoying situations of the relationship, supporting you navigate the complexities of the connection and extend extra healthful coping techniques.

They also can allow you to broaden a plan for breaking unfastened from the dynamic and constructing a more in shape, greater enjoyable life for your self as nicely.

Developing internal electricity and resilience is key to overcoming a narcissist. Not to appears like a damaged report but constructing a help network, training self-care, placing boundaries, learning to recognize gaslighting, building vanity, running in the direction of assertiveness, and seeking out professional assist are all strategies with a purpose to can help you navigate the demanding situations of being in a dating with a narcissist or to ultimately ruin loose from the dynamic. Remember, you can't alternate the narcissist, however you could exchange the way you reply to them and take back control of your personal properly-being.

Case Study: "Cindy" and "Mark"

Cindy had constantly felt like some thing changed into off in her marriage to Mark, but she couldn't pretty positioned her finger on what it have become. At first, she had belief it have end up clearly the strain in their traumatic jobs and busy schedules. But as time went on, she started out to recognize that there has been some component greater occurring.

Mark had usually been very essential of Cindy, and nothing she did seemed to be wonderful sufficient for him. He might also continuously nitpick at her, asserting her flaws and mistakes. Even whilst subjects were going properly, he ought to find a few component to complain approximately.

Over time, Cindy started to revel in like she become on foot on eggshells round Mark. She emerge as constantly on side, looking in advance to the subsequent criticism or grievance. She began to doubt herself and her talents, and perplexed if she modified into as incompetent as Mark appeared to anticipate.

Despite her growing experience of unease, Cindy attempted to make topics work. She went out of her manner to attempt to please Mark, hoping that if she ought to in reality get subjects proper, he could ultimately be satisfied. But no matter what she did, it turn out to be in no way sufficient.

As time went on, the grievance and blame great grew worse. Mark started to turn out to be an increasing number of controlling, on the lookout for to dictate every problem of Cindy's lifestyles. He may tell her what to area on, who she ought to speak to, and wherein she have to go. Cindy felt like she changed into suffocating below his regular watchful eye.

One day, after a horrible argument, wherein Mark had blamed her for a few aspect that wasn't her fault, Cindy finally reached her breaking point. She located out that regardless of what she did, Mark emerge as in no manner going to be satisfied. He may want to constantly discover some thing to complain about in a few manner to make her enjoy small and insignificant.

With profound unhappiness, Cindy made the hard choice to leave her empty, unloving marriage after all the years she had spent together with her husband. It wasn't an smooth choice—she cherished Mark, or the individual that she perception she knew to be Mark, however she knew that staying with him modified into excellent going to make her enjoy worse ultimately. She identified that Mark changed into in no way going to exchange, but she realized that she had, and to her gain. She had ultimately placed the inner energy to leave him. She deserved loads more.

After she left, Cindy commenced out the method of slowly rebuilding her life. It wasn't clean—she had to find out a contemporary region to live, a latest process, and a contemporary revel in of motive. But over time, she commenced to experience like herself yet again.

Looking again over her marriage to Mark, Cindy found out that she had been a sufferer of narcissistic abuse and had been from the very starting of their courting; she had just refused to recall it. Mark had used blame and complaint to govern her, making her revel in like she have come to be constantly within the wrong. It had taken her a long term to see thru his manipulations, however in the end, she modified into succesful to interrupt loose and discover a new enjoy of strength and resilience. She have become ready to fulfill her new life head-on. The grieving that she felt for Mark had already been skilled for decades and it changed into now time for her to transport on.

Conclusion

Healing and Recovery

Recovering from a narcissistic relationship may be a hard and complex approach. It requires self-meditated photograph, emotional healing, and growing healthy relationship patterns.

Remember the following as you work to regain resilience and your freedom:

Recognize the narcissistic dating: The first step is to well known that you had been in a narcissistic dating. Understand the dispositions and patterns of narcissistic conduct, consisting of manipulation, lack of empathy, and a feel of entitlement.

Cut off contact: Establishing no contact or minimal contact with the narcissistic character is vital. This lets in create a steady place for healing and prevents in addition manipulation or abuse.

Seek manual: Reach out to depended on friends, own family contributors, or a therapist who can offer help and steerage at some point of the healing device. Support corporations in particular for survivors of narcissistic abuse additionally may be useful.

Educate your self: Learn more approximately narcissism, codependency, and healthy relationship dynamics. Understanding those thoughts will assist you gain belief into your stories and empower you to make more healthy options shifting ahead.

Practice self-care: Prioritize self-care sports sports that sell your physical, emotional, and intellectual nicely-being. Engage in sports activities you enjoy, workout relaxation techniques, exercising often, and ensure you have got got become enough rest and nutrients.

Process your feelings: Allow yourself to grieve and heal from the emotional wounds as a result of the narcissistic relationship. This might also comprise expressing this via remedy.

Set barriers: Establish clean obstacles to shield your self from destiny toxic relationships. Learn to understand and assert your desires, speak correctly, and say no whilst crucial. Surround your self with folks who appreciate your barriers.

Build self-esteem: Rebuild your conceitedness and self-worth via way of focusing in your strengths, accomplishments, and tremendous functions. Challenge bad self-speak and workout selfcompassion and self-love.

Rediscover your identity: Reconnect together collectively together with your interests, passions, and goals. Rediscovering your non-public identity outside of the narcissistic relationship is crucial for private increase and shifting forward.

Foster wholesome relationships: Once you have got healed and acquired resilience, you may start searching for wholesome, loving relationships.

What a Healthy Relationship Looks Like

If you've been caught inside the cycle of narcissistic abuse, it may be tough to recognise what a healthful relationship includes.

Here are the property you should look for in a modern day courting:

Mutual recognize: Both companions treat each one in all a type with admire, kindness, and hobby. There is a lack of energy imbalances or emotional manipulation.

Effective communication: Open and sincere conversation is valued, and each companions actively take note of each different. Conflict is addressed constructively and with a willingness to discover a preference.

Emotional assist: Both companions provide emotional useful resource and validation to every one-of-a-type. They are empathetic and knowledge, and everybody's feelings and dreams are valued.

Trust and honesty: Trust is mounted thru steady and sincere conduct. There isn't any want for secrecy or deception in a healthful dating.

Independence and interdependence: Each partner maintains their individuality and has their personal interests, interests, and goals. At the same time, there is a experience of interdependence, wherein each partners manual and rely upon each one-of-a-kind in a balanced way.

Shared values and dreams: Healthy relationships comprise shared values, desires, and visions for the destiny. Both partners are dedicated to the relationship and paintings together within the path of common dreams.

Love: Love is affected individual, accepting, understanding, empathetic, strong, and secure.

Ask yourself the ones very last following questions on your dating:Do you have got sensible expectancies approximately each other?

Do you feel like you have got were given a remarkable partnership with every different?Do you and your beloved experience each one-of-a-kind's organization?

Does your giant notable positioned your needs in advance than theirs even as it is desired?

Do you experience strong whilst you are with them?

Does it sense which includes you every are growing and maturing within the dating?

Do you believe each exclusive?

If you spoke back positive to maximum of those questions, then you definitely honestly maximum in all likelihood have a loving relationship. Remember there may be no nice courting. But if you could't say tremendous to maximum of these questions, don't forget what you need going ahead together with your lifestyles. Live your existence the manner you need it to be lived.

Remember that restoration from a narcissistic courting takes time and staying power. It's crucial to prioritize your well-being and are looking for for expert help if you may. Recovering from emotional and intellectual abuse requires assist, information, and time.

Take your first step right now and make the willpower to start constructing the inspiration for your existence and a extra healthful, happier you!

A Call to Action! If you have determined this e-book a beneficial beneficial resource for each you or someone you recognize, it is probably extensively desired if you may depart your evaluation on Amazon.Com so that others is probably helped. My circle of relatives thanks you for it!